Bullying, Suicide, and Homicide

Bullying, Suicide, and Homicide

Understanding, Assessing,
and Preventing Threats to Self and
Others for Victims of Bullying

Butch Losey

Routledge
Taylor & Francis Group
New York London

Routledge
Taylor & Francis Group
711 Third Avenue
New York, NY 10017

Routledge
Taylor & Francis Group
27 Church Road
Hove, East Sussex BN3 2FA

Printed in the United States of America on acid-free paper
10 9 8 7 6 5 4 3 2 1

International Standard Book Number: 978-0-415-87344-4 (Hardback) 978-0-415-87347-5 (Paperback)

Library of Congress Cataloging-in-Publication Data

Losey, Butch.
  Bullying, suicide, and homicide : understanding, assessing, and preventing
threats to self and others for victims of bullying / Butch Losey.
    p. cm.
  Includes bibliographical references and index.
  ISBN 978-0-415-87344-4 (hardcover : alk. paper) -- ISBN 978-0-415-87347-5
(pbk. : alk. paper)
  1. Bullying. 2. Bullying--Prevention. 3. Suicide. 4. Homicide. I. Title.

BF637.B85L67 2011
302.3--dc22   2010047313

Visit the Taylor & Francis Web site at
http://www.taylorandfrancis.com

and the Routledge Web site at
http://www.routledgementalhealth.com

Contents

V

CONTENTS

Preface

I was like many others: a victim of bullying. My story has no tragic end or great triumph over adversity. It happened; I suffered to some degree and somehow navigated the experience through avoidance or fighting back. Beyond that, I have no real personal story of bullying to tell.

Some years back, many things seemed to converge all at once in my life. I was struggling to finish a doctoral degree and trying to figure out how to collect data for ethnographic research on the importance of family dinners. I was going nowhere with it. At the suggestion of my boss, I switched my research to collecting data on the Olweus Bullying Prevention Program, a program that I had recently been certified to teach and was set to implement in four schools in a local district.

School had been in session for just over a month when we began the implementation of the Olweus program, and I concurrently began my data collection. During this time, I was asked to assist in the implementation in several schools of another prevention-based program called the Signs of Suicide. For this program, we surveyed every student in the schools and then conducted a personal interview with any student who was identified as a suicide risk. I was astounded by the number of children who reported that they had or were contemplating suicide to some degree because of the bullying they were experiencing. Surprisingly, we had never asked about bullying during the survey.

As I worked on both projects, I was regularly contacted by schools interested in implementing bullying prevention and parents trying to figure out how to stop their child from being victimized. I also heard from a few people who had lost loved ones tragically by suicide as a way to escape the pain of bullying. As they talked, I listened. Their stories touched me. I learned the connection among bullying, suicide, and school violence. I learned of our failures in mental health and education to protect these children.

I wondered what I could do to make a difference. I decided that I could help by filling in a gap and creating a way to assess the impact of bullying victimization on mental health. I expected that by using a screening and assessment tool with victims of bullying, a mental health professional could identify the level of torment a child was experiencing and in this way potentially divert the tragic solution of suicide or school violence some children choose. Using these tools could get the student the help they need.

Bullying, Suicide, and Homicide will increase your understanding of the impact of bullying on the core essence of one's sense of self. You will learn that bullying prevention and intervention will be most successful when an ecological approach is implemented. You will learn the components of screening and assessment tools that will guide your decision-making process as you intervene with victims of bullying. All the tools and forms that I have created are printed as appendices and are on the CD included with this book. The CD will afford you the opportunity to modify the tools to fit your individual work setting.

I believe that I have met my goal for making a difference. Professionals across the country are using these tools. I have presented numerous workshops on the topic. And—you are reading this book. *Bullying, Suicide, and Homicide* will add to your repertoire of skills to intervene during a difficult time in a young person's life. Your intervention may translate into one life saved. That difference is in no small measure what I had hoped to accomplish.

Acknowledgments

I would like to recognize and thank Susan Graham for her ideas that contributed to the development of the Bullying Lethality Screening Tool. The screening tool created the foundation for the material in this book. I would also like to thank Jim Carter, chief executive officer of Child Focus Incorporated, for his continued support of my bullying prevention efforts. Both are strong advocates for bullying prevention in Cincinnati, Ohio.

Author's Note

Many writers on bullying go to great lengths to be sensitive to labeling individuals. They are careful to avoid using the terms *bully* and *victim* as much as possible when describing students who bully others or who are bullied by others. I depart from this perspective to respect the experience of those who have been the victim of a persistent, unwanted, and seriously harmful assault on their physical, emotional, and psychological essence of self. Bullying is victimization; therefore, bullies have victims.

PERSISTENT BULLYING AND SUICIDE AS A VIABLE OPTION

Desire''s car sits in the garage as if it is waiting for her to drive down Bach Buxton with the windows down and her hair blowing in the wind. Her room sits the way she left it, as if waiting for her return. I too sometimes lose track of reality and think she will be coming through the front door any minute.

Donna Dreyer, mother of Desire' Dreyer

Moving to a New School

When Desire'[1] first transferred to Eastside High School[2] outside Cincinnati, Ohio, the eighth grader was full of promise. The attractive blond had trained as a cheerleader since she was seven and was eager to pick up with the sport at her new school. Like any teenager, she had trepidation about moving, yet this was a girl with many talents, a strong academic record, and a disarming smile. She was sure to adapt.

The transition to her new school would have appeared relatively smooth to anyone willing to notice in the hustle of the middle school milieu, yet a seemingly insignificant event would open the door to a perception of persecution that Desire' believed was orchestrated by Eastside High. She also would soon be in a downward emotional

---

[1] Desire' Dreyer (2007). Adapted from personal interviews with Donna Dreyer, Desire''s mother. Some of the elements of the story have been added for readability.
[2] Eastside and Westside schools and individual names other than Desire' and her family are fictitious names to maintain anonymity.

Desire´ Dreyer

spiral and experience escalating abuse by her peers that continued over the course of the next several years.

Desire´ adjusted quickly to Eastside High and signed up for tryouts for the cheerleading squad. Desire´ was caught off guard when told by the school counselor that she "held all zeros" on her report card from Kentucky and was ineligible to try out for cheerleading. Desire´ was devastated, knowing that the zeros reflected a glitch in transferring her grades from her school in Newport, Kentucky, just across the river from Cincinnati. However, she interpreted the situation as a sign that the school administration did not want her.

Within just a few weeks of starting school, Desire´ made several friends and developed a close relationship with Ashley, a girl her age. She also began a romantic relationship with a boy she met at the Eastside versus Westside basketball game. Her relationship with Cameron would become a source of support and affection and the catalyst for victimizing Desire´. Finally, her grades from Newport were forwarded, and she would qualify and compete with the junior varsity cheerleading squad through the end of eighth grade.

At the end of her ninth-grade year, Desire´ decided to transfer to the communications and technology program at Westside High School; driving her decision certainly was the knowledge that Cameron was at Westside. The decision would require her to meet class prerequisites, and she decided to complete these during the summer. Along with the typical activities of a teen with a summer free, Desire´ completed the necessary paperwork to transfer to Westside and attended summer classes.

Several days before the start of school, Desire´ received a call from the school counselor at Westside informing her that her application was denied, and she would not be placed in the communications and technology program because the student enrollment maximum had been reached. Desire´ was devastated once again, concluding that this was the second time the school district had intentionally hurt her. She talked to her parents, and her father brought the issue to the superintendent. Following a meeting with the superintendent, the school counselor informed Desire´ that she would be admitted to the program. It was too late, however, because Desire´ had settled on an impression of the school; she was not welcome at Westside.

Tenth grade offered great possibilities for Desire´. She entered Westside's communication and technology program with enthusiasm. She was thrilled being with her boyfriend and had made the junior varsity football cheerleading squad. The coming tempest gained strength in the form of jealousy and teen competition.

The Genesis of Cruelty

Amber Gavin, another girl on the junior varsity squad, initially presented herself as a friend to Desire´ and gained her trust. Her latent motive was to keep track of Desire´ as she pursued Cameron, Desire´'s boyfriend. Amber was jealous of Desire´ and Cameron's relationship and was intent on breaking them up. When this did not work, she resorted to frequent emotional and physical threats. There were times when Desire´ actually believed some of the horrid comments and threats that Amber said to and about her.

"I will kill you!" was written on the note posted on Desire´'s locker. "You are not worthy of Cameron; you are worthless." The written threat was followed up with a confrontation in the hallway when Amber told Desire´ that several girls were planning to attack her after cheerleading practice. Desire´ called her mother by cell phone, who in turn contacted the school coach. He assured Mrs. Dreyer that no harm would come to Desire´. Her mother also contacted the police department, which in effect would be the first of many reports to the police department. Desire´'s parents had a casual meeting with Amber's parents at the Gavin home, and it was decided to keep the children apart. All these strategies did stop the aggression temporarily.

In the fall, Desire´ was fortunate to qualify for the varsity cheerleading squad, squeezing out Melanie Richards, a girl who had been in cheerleading as long as Desire´ and who most thought was a guaranteed member of the team. Melanie was placed on the junior varsity squad, and this led to a resurgence of aggression toward Desire´.

Desire´ began to struggle with her grades in the fall of that year, and Mrs. Dreyer became concerned yet did not make the connection that the grades were related to the bullying. Desire´ began hanging out with several different girls who seemed to perpetuate a "bad girl" persona. Maybe this was Desire´'s method of protecting herself.

Mrs. Dreyer asked the school counselor to talk with Desire´ and Cameron in hopes of understanding Desire´'s drastic drop in grades and her increasingly depressed and angry mood. The school counselor responded a few days later that everything was fine because Desire´ was positive about school and was making plans for college. She told Mrs. Dreyer that she could not understand what would be causing such a drop in school performance.

Early October brought homecoming, and Desire´ and Cameron enjoyed the evening together. They returned to Desire´'s parent's home and sat down for a little while with Mr. and Mrs. Dreyer. The evening was interrupted when Amber and two of her friends began shouting obscenities in the front yard. Desire´ and Cameron went outside, as did the Dreyers, and the girls continued to threaten and call Desire´ names. They refused to leave the property when Mr. Dreyer asked them, and they continued to threaten Desire´. Ultimately, the confrontation ended when Cameron pushed Amber toward her car, and Amber left threatening to sue the Dreyer family.

The following weekend, the same group of girls waited to ambush Desire´ as she returned from cheerleading an "away" game. As was typical, the cheerleaders and their families were en route to Applebee's, where they would have dinner following the game. Desire´ drove in her car, followed some distance behind by Mr. and Mrs. Dreyer.

Mr. Dreyer answered his cell phone just moments prior to arriving at Applebee's. Desire´ was screaming hysterically on the phone "Where are you?" she asked, stating that she desperately needed him. Desire´ had parked at Applebee's, and Amber and a group of girls had surrounded her car and were threatening her. She was locked in her car and had called the police. Moments later, Mr. and Mrs. Dreyer arrived, and the girls ran to their cars and left the parking lot; however, this was not before Amber screamed, "We will get you, you bitch." When the police arrived, the police officer refused to take a report, stating that they would like the family to talk to the school resource officer at Westside High School.

The Final Blow

Bullying Desire´ was in full swing by the New Year's Eve party. Twenty minutes after arriving, Desire´ was invited into one of the smaller bedrooms of the host home by Amber and two other girls, Susan and Brooke, girls who chose their friends based on the degree of benefit to them. Amber pulled out a small cigarette case and a piece of plastic tubing; from the case, Amber drew out a small, rolled-up white bag containing fine-powdered cocaine. She used the tube to draw a strong sniff of a line of the white powder from the cover of the case and then offered the case and tube to Desire´. Desire´ walked away without comment, and as she walked away, Amber began calling her names and teasing her.

Desire´ had brought both Susan and Brooke to the party and now planned to leave them. She went into the kitchen to get her belongings to leave and was confronted by Brooke, who asked her not to leave because she would not have a ride home. Desire´ said that she was leaving, and if she or Susan wanted a ride, they would have to leave now. Brooke said that she would not leave, and Desire´ left through the front door. As she drove away, Desire´ could see the three girls from the rearview mirror; they were laughing and then turned back into the house.

The abuse gained in intensity following the New Year's Eve party. Regularly, the girls would call and text message Desire´ with threats to kill her. For several weeks, Desire´ was threatened by phone and text messages every 10 minutes after school hours. Sometimes, it would go on for many hours.

Amber, Susan, and Brooke now began to harass her even in class. They threw empty water bottles at her, shot spitballs at her, and pulled her hair. This happened in the presence of the teacher when the teacher was not facing the class or when she left the classroom.

Suicide as a Viable Option

Amber, Susan, and Brooke chased Desire´ down the hallway through the hustle of children during change of classes. Desire´ ran into the restroom and locked herself in the stall farthest from the doorway.

"We will kill you, you whore," Brooke threatened as she stood in the doorway holding the door open to the restroom. "If it doesn't happen here, we will get you at home or at cheerleading. You can't hide."

Desire´ called her mother as she sat crying on the floor of the girl's restroom. She cried hysterically for about 30 minutes until she went to the principal's office as her mother suggested. The principal called Desire´ and the girls in to his office and told them all to stop the drama, and that if they did not, they would all be suspended from school for 3 days. Desire´ wrote a small note to her friend during the next class on a piece of paper torn from the back of one of her textbooks:

> They blamed it all on me. Mr. Jones told them that if anyone said one word as they walked out of the office it would be a three-day suspension. What do you know, the second they left, Ashley, it was like, I swear, I want to hit something or someone, they didn't do shit. No I don't know if I will be able to switch classes or not, so I think I will be changing schools or something and you know that they're not going to stop anyway.

Life seemed to slowly close in around Desire´ in an isolating cloud of torment, fear, and self-blame from the actions of those who would later mourn her loss. She sat in her room on the third day absent from school because she was sick, what her mother would later describe as "silent pain." She read the text message sent from Amber. "You are worthless and no one, including Cameron, wants you, so you might as well kill yourself." She likely saw little originality in Amber's suggestion since Desire´ had probably thought about suicide on many occasions and may have practiced the scenario about as many times.

She sent a text message to her friend Michelle: "I love Cameron."

She sent a text message to her friend Gabby: "I love Cameron."

She sent a text message to her friend Ashley: "Just tell me, who is saying it, and what are they saying?"

She walked to her bedroom and gathered the small box of items that she had collected methodically over the past several months and placed it on the dining room table. Desire´ then tied the rope securely and placed her neck through the noose, lowering herself as she struggled. Life ended for Desire´ that afternoon by her choice of one undesirable option—an option considered, practiced, and set aside until that day—one ending with death but surely more about escape.

From Tragedy to Prevention

Our society too often views bullying as an irritable but inescapable part of growing up, as if it is a stage that we all go through in childhood. Bullying has somehow earned its standing as a behavior that falls somehow in its own legal and social category. Bullying is fairly similar to another behavior with another name, yet that behavior is punishable by considerable jail time and carries a much greater social stigma. That behavior is called child abuse. Rarely are bullies punished using legal statutes, and punishment is most often determined by schools that claim there is little punishment that they can actually dole out. In the case of Desire´, none of the girls was held accountable for her actions. Her mother chose not to file a civil lawsuit because she did not want to suffer the anguish of going through a trial. She was also not that confident the lawsuit would be successful.

One of the many lessons learned from Desire´'s tragic story is that there was a missing piece in the prevention and intervention system for this school district. The school personnel were not prepared to assess the bullying Desire´ was experiencing or adequately able to offer her mental health intervention in the context of bullying. I am glad to say that following the tragedy of Desire´'s death, the school district implemented policy changes, established a districtwide bullying prevention program, and trained all of the school staff (and some nonschool staff) on bullying prevention and intervention.

It is the goal of this book to describe in detail my process for addressing metal health referrals for children who are experiencing bullying and are experiencing suicidal ideation or threatening violence. My process is composed of three comprehensive stages; screen, assess, and mediate (SAM). The first stage, *screen,* utilizes the Bullying Lethality Screening Tool that I cocreated with my colleague Susan Graham. This screen helps identify the "red flags" for bullying, depression, isolation, suicide, and school violence. The second stage is *assess,* and this stage is a process of assessing suicide and threats of violence using two assessment tools that guide the mental health professional through the process. The third section, *mediate,* identifies interventions for persistent bullying or when a determination is made that risk is imminent for suicide or school violence.

Before anyone can determine risk, it will be important to have a thorough understanding of the nature of bullying, its impact, and the risk factors of bullying, suicide, and school violence. It will also be important to understand the foundations of bullying prevention in schools. For this reason, I spend some time in the opening chapters developing these topics to support the later chapters related to the SAM process.

2

EFFECTIVE SCHOOL PREVENTION

Some of the kids knew about it before it happened, but they
didn't want to say anything—they have a code of honor and they
did not want to tattletale. But someone has to stand up; someone
has to take a stand because, if you don't, then somebody else is
going to get hurt.

Gregory Carter, Teacher, Richmond, Virginia
Victim of a school shooting

The research shows that one in five children in primary and secondary schools is the victim of some type of bullying. Conflict between
peers, including bullying behavior, aggression, and physical violence,
begins in preschool and persists throughout the school years. Studies
have consistently found that a substantial number of schoolchildren
are the victims of bullying, and although levels of bullying vary, some
estimates indicate that schools will have no less than 19% of their
population reporting incidents of bullying at some time during the
school term (Nansel et al., 2001; Whitney & Smith, 1991).

On the prevalence of bullying behavior, I draw from my own
research through a survey I conducted in Clermont County, Ohio
(Losey & Graham, 2004). In 2003, while working at Child Focus
Incorporated, a community mental health agency on the east side of
Cincinnati, our staff surveyed students in seven Clermont County
elementary schools across three districts to assess the prevalence of
bullying behavior in the schools of our community. The survey was
administered in 33 homeroom classrooms to 630 students in Grades
3–6. Almost half of the students surveyed reported that they had been
bullied two or three times per month. One fourth of the students surveyed reported that they had bullied someone else two or three times
per month. This is much higher than our national average of around

19%, and I believe this is due to the district at the time lacking a consistent effort in bullying prevention.

Some people view private schools differently, believing that these schools are a refuge from bullying, and that bullying is more an element of the public school system. In April 2009, I conducted a survey at a small private school in Cincinnati. The survey was administered to 287 children in Grades 3–8. Surprising to their staff, 23% of the students reported being bullied two or three times a month, which is slightly above a national comparison of about 19%.

With bullying so prevalent in the school system, it is critical that prevention efforts are focused on the population in which it is occurring and the location where it takes place. Understandably, bullying occurs across the life span and in a variety of locations, even though it could be argued that bullying is most prevalent during the school age years and within the school environment. Since this book is about children, prevention, and intervention in the schools, I focus my discussion here on this population and location.

Levels of Ecology

Almost three quarters of a century ago, Kurt Lewin (1936) proposed his well-known equation $B = f(P \times E)$ in his book *Principles of Topological Psychology*. It is not a mathematical equation, but an equation that describes a social construct. Simply stated, it means that the behavior (B) can be seen as a function (f) of a person's (P) interaction with his or her environment (E). From this equation, the ecological model was born.

Years later, Urie Bronfenbrenner (1977) added to our ecological understanding by describing what he called his evolving scientific perspective of the ecology of human development. Most important from this article was his four levels of ecological contexts, which he called systems (Table 2.1).

These moved from the most near to the person to the most distant. Bronfenbrenner named these systems the microsystem (relations between the person and environment in the immediate setting containing that person); the mesosystem (the interaction among major settings containing the person, such as interaction between family

Table 2.1　Bronfenbrenner's Levels of Ecological Context

Microsystem	Primary setting, containing person
Mesosystem	Interaction between two microsystems
Exosystem	Influencing system not containing person
Macrosystem	Broader culture

Source: From Bronfenbrenner, U. (1977). *American Psychologist, 32,* 513–531.

and school or family and church); the exosystem (contexts that are an extension of the mesosystem but do not contain the person but effect and influence the immediate settings in which that person is found); and the macrosystem (the institutional patterns of the culture or subculture, such as the economic, social, educational, and legal, that have an impact on behavior and meaning making).

Ecological Interventions

An ecological approach to bullying prevention should use a full range of intervention targets that occur simultaneously on different levels of the ecology (Conyne & Cook, 2004) from the microlevel to the macrolevel. From an ecological perspective, one of the criteria for evaluating the impact of interventions is whether the intervention has increased the resources of the school where they are implemented. This can be seen through improvements in school policy, increasing bullying prevention skills for staff, increasing students' social competency, or adding bullying prevention curriculum to the faculty library. The critical feature of increasing the resources of the school is whether the school is able to follow through on the intervention, which is no easy task. Because the transfer of skills is so important from the ecological perspective, it is important that interventions are created using current research in the field of bullying prevention and that people on site are involved in the creation and delivery of the interventions.

This does not commonly occur, however. In a large study of research on prevention programs (Durlak & Wells, 1997), it was observed that many interventions were delivered by people outside the setting where they occurred. These were usually mental health professionals and college students; this raises the question of whether it would be difficult for those resources to remain after the intervention is finished.

In the rest of this chapter, I discuss what I believe should be goals of bullying prevention and intervention for each of the four main ecological levels. I have also added the chronosystem level and discuss the effects of time on prevention. Keep in mind that the overarching goal is to increase the resources of the staff and students of the school.

Microsystem

Bullying is contextual, and in the case of school bullying, 85% of bullying incidents occur in the context of peers (Pepler & Craig, 2000) at the microsystem level. In the broader context, bullying comes from problems in school climate and is not simply a student's response to a particular environment (e.g., school) but is better described as an interaction between the peer group and the environment. Therefore, intervention must target the environment and the peer group (Table 2.2).

Microsystem influences include the actual interaction among the bully, victim, and bystanders. An obvious intervention that targets the microsystem would be an immediate intervention with the bully and the victim "in the moment" of the interaction. An example of this is the teacher stopping the bullying in progress, instructing the bully to stop, and telling the bystanders to behave differently. Another example is for the school counselor to work directly with the victim to develop skills or strategize to make a change in behavior.

Empower Victims and Bystanders

Empowerment of the victim and bystanders can be accomplished by education and skill development. Victim and bystander should be educated on the nature of bullying and the bullying prevention efforts of the school. Social skill development in areas such as assertiveness,

Table 2.2 Goals at the Microlevel

Empower victims and bystanders
Increase effective leadership
Develop competency in staff intervention
Increase support and individual resources
Change accepting attitudes of bullying and violence

social awareness, or social skill training will be particularly important for both the victim and bystanders.

I do make the distinction between social skill training and social awareness training. Social awareness training is most helpful for provocative victims who tend to miss the cues from other students and school staff. They are trained to notice and critique how others respond to their behavior. Social skills training would teach and model specific social skills to the student, with the student rehearsing the skills with the teacher and then the teacher offering honest feedback to the student on his or her use of the skill. The goal is to increase the student's repertoire of skills and develop competency in the skills that are taught.

Students will also need knowledge of how to access the system to prevent and report bullying. It is important that all the students in the school have knowledge and understanding of how to access the resources and people of the school. Ultimately, increasing skills at this level will help the victim be assertive and seek help and for the bystander to act in some way to stop the bullying, by either safely intervening or reporting the incidents to others who can help.

Increase Effective Leadership

Leadership at the microsystem level includes the principal and other administrators of the school. In the course of my dissertation, I learned that leadership can make or break a prevention program. In my study, I had two schools in the same district with similar student populations implementing the same bullying prevention program. A noticeable difference was the leadership styles of the principals. One principal was highly effective in communicating the goals of the prevention program and following up to ensure tasks were completed. The other principal did not provide enough direction and communication to the prevention team. This was interpreted by the faculty and staff as the principal appearing unsupportive of the prevention efforts. This ultimately reduced the effectiveness of the bullying prevention program.

It is necessary to have administrative support and, truly, an inspirational and effective leader who can pull together the internal resources and strengths necessary to support the development of an intervention that will live well beyond its creation.

Develop Competency in Staff Intervention

When a bullying prevention program begins at school, it is important that staff respond immediately in all situations of bullying. If this does not happen, students get the message that nothing has changed and may get the impression that staff are either okay with the behavior or do not know what to do about it.

As staff consistently responds to bullying situations, students understand that it is important to intervene. Staff modeling may lead to students coming to the aid of victimized students because there will be a sense of safety that staff will intervene.

School staff will need to be effective in their communication with each other. There will be a need to report bullying incidents to other staff and a means of accessing this information quickly so that staff can understand the extent to which a student is being bullied or bullying others. This would include reporting of any consequences that may have been imposed, interventions that have been tried, parent interaction, and individual plans created with students.

Increase Support and Individual Resources

Students who are excluded, disconnected, or in some way viewed differently are highly susceptible to victimization and need the support of staff and students. I believe that it is the responsibility of everyone (staff, students, and nonteaching staff) in the school to include all students in the activities of school. I tell students that this does not mean that they need to be best friends with everyone, but it is their responsibility to include other students in school activities, such as work groups and sports activities in physical education; yes, it would be nice if they included others in conversation at lunchtime.

Increasing positive adult relationships in the school setting can offer considerable support for students. It is important that students feel they have an adult in the school with whom they have a positive relationship and who is available to them. This does not necessarily need to be one of the teaching staff. I remember being in grade school and the strong positive influence Mr. Culbertson, our school custodian, was for many of us boys.

Another way to view bullying of others is to consider it in terms of peer influence. I ask students to evaluate how they influence their peers. I acknowledge that kids who bully make a choice to influence in destructive ways. I like to remind kids, particularly the popular ones, to use their influence wisely and positively. It is easy to see how just one or two bullies can influence the school climate and make the environment an unsafe place; I remind everyone that the same principle applies if students utilize their influence positively.

Some students will need even more support. In the schools where I work, we typically have mental health prevention workers who serve on a bullying prevention committee. The professionals support students by creating individualized behavior plans and working with students on bullying issues on a regular basis.

One of the most difficult times of the day for victims of bullying is during transitional times and times of less structure. Having staff increase observation and monitoring during lunchroom periods and playground activities and in hallways during transition is a supportive strategy that creates safety and helps students see that staff are in charge.

Students need to learn new skills, practice new skills, develop empathy, and hear the challenges and successes of fellow students. Many prevention programs do this by having a specific time of the day when classroom-level meetings are conducted. Dan Olweus (1993) recommended that these meetings happen weekly and, depending on the age of the students, be 20–45 minutes long. Having implemented bullying prevention programs in many schools, the classroom meeting is the one component of bullying prevention that I regularly hear from students and faculty as having a significant influence on school behavior and connectedness.

Change the Accepting Attitudes of Bullying and Violence

Accepting attitudes of bullying can be subtle yet corrosive. I frequently hear accepting and complacent attitudes as I offer workshops on bullying prevention. Some people believe that bullying is just a part of growing up, and that there is little that you can do but get through it. Others believe that violence should be met with violence. I have also heard the stories of adults who talk about when they grew up and the successes of stopping bullying by getting a group of kids to attack and hurt the bully.

These beliefs are inaccurate. Bullying is not a part of growing up, and it is not true that with successful navigation of bullying children will become better adults. It is also not useful to attack violence with violence. Typically, bullies choose their victims by some imbalance of power; with boys, this is often physical strength. Children who fight back are likely only going to cause themselves more harm. That does not mean that they cannot be assertive, but they certainly should not consider violence.

Mesosystem

The mesosystem is the interaction of two or more microsystems. Examples of mesosystems include interaction between family and school, such as parent–teacher collaboration; interaction of the family and the legal system; and collaboration between school and a place of student employment. The primary mesosystem in school bullying prevention is the school–parent mesosystem. There are number of goals for intervention at this level (Table 2.3).

Educate Parents on Bullying and Bullying Prevention Efforts

Schools can intervene on the mesosystem level first by educating students and families on the nature of bullying and the prevention efforts

Table 2.3   Goals at the Mesolevel

Educate parents about bullying and bullying prevention program
Regular communication with parents
Report incidents of bullying and victimization
Encourage community building
Work with parents of involved students
Involve parents in school prevention planning and activities

and policies of the school. Parents should understand whether data were collected and what that means to the school, how the school is responding to the data, and what the projected outcomes of the prevention program are. Data collection and follow-up with parents and other stakeholders at the end of the school year would be important to show successes and plans for the next year.

Parents should also understand the internal workings of the program. These include the interventions that will be utilized, the rules and consequences concerning bullying and school violence, and how parents will be informed of situations as they arise.

Regular Communication With Parents

The old adage that an ounce of prevention equals a pound of cure would go a long way when communicating with parents. Parents are greatly distressed when they feel that they are hearing for the first time of their child being bullied despite evidence that bullying has been going on for quite some time. Communicating all bullying situations to parents will help them make critical decisions regarding their children's safety and welfare.

Schools that are successful at ongoing communication with parents use a variety of methods to keep them informed. They use traditional and contemporary means of communicating. They report progress through one-page reports posted on their Web sites, send monthly newsletters on bullying prevention through the e-mail marketing tool Constant Contact, and send video clip links of student-developed infomercials through YouTube.

Report Incidents of Bullying and Victimization

For any situation in which a student has bullied another or has been victimized, notification is important, and the parents of both the bully and the victim should be advised. The school should report the circumstances of this situation, the school's response, any discipline that was applied, and techniques provided for students to change their behavior (in the case of bullying) or to access help, report, or respond effectively to bullying (in the case of victimization).

Reporting to local law enforcement should also be considered. Many bullying situations cross the line between school bullying that can be addressed in the principal's office and criminal behavior. A good mesosystem interaction is one of regular contact with law enforcement or, better yet, a school resource officer.

Encourage Community Building

Another activity of the mesosystem is community building. Schools that have high levels of support, belongingness, trust, and cooperation contribute to positive socioemotional and behavioral outcomes (Maton, 1999). Community-building activities enhance the ability of students to work together for a common purpose in work, social groups, or organizations. A sense of community occurs when students are in charge, can have the power to set the rules and standards, and ultimately work together to accomplish shared goals (Naparstek, 1999).

Work With Parents of Involved Students

Effective communication will be critical in how staff convey issues of bullying and victimization with parents. An effective strategy that I have found is to help the parent understand that school personnel and the parent have a common goal, which is to provide the best school experience for their child. Inviting the parent to help meet this goal and be a part of the process of addressing a particular issue can be successful in reducing resistance and blame, particularly when you are calling a parent to discuss his or her child's bullying behavior. Calls home to parents are also a great way to educate the parents on bullying prevention efforts.

Involve Parents in School Prevention Planning and Activities

I recently worked with a school that had an initiative to have a father or grandfather participate in school activities for a full day, every day of the school year. In essence, there would be an adult male volunteer at the school every day of the school year. These men would be in the classroom helping students with their work, attending lunch, and assisting with gym and recess. The strategy was initially introduced to get more male parent involvement in the school, but they found that the strategy increased positive behavior in the classroom; they planned to make the initiative a regular part of the school curriculum. Schools could take this strategy a step further and involve parents on planning committees for bullying prevention and as part of a volunteer program that supports bullying prevention efforts.

Exosystem

Table 2.4 presents interventions to utilize at the exosystem level. These interventions are discussed next.

Create Understanding of Baseline Behavior

Bronfenbrenner (1977) states that the exosystem is an extension of the mesosystem, but that it does not contain the student. It could, however, have a significant impact on them. A beginning exosystem intervention is to make an assessment of the nature and prevalence of bullying at the school. Schools typically do this by surveying students and staff regarding the prevalence and type of bullying in school. This is important because prevention efforts will be focused on data collected. Data typically collected include the students' perceptions of types of bullying, types of victimization, locations where there are many incidents of bullying behavior, and responses by adults. The survey that is accepted by many researchers and schools is Dan Olweus's Bullying Victim Questionnaire (Olweus, 2001). Other schools monitor bullying incident density by having adults observe and tally bullying behavior in specific locations.

Table 2.4   Goals at the Exolevel

Create understanding of baseline behavior
Develop bullying prevention policy and procedures
Develop a bullying prevention committee to drive prevention program
Train all school staff
Use internal and external experts

Develop Bullying Prevention Policy and Procedures

I recommend that schools first make the decision to create a bullying policy and not position it in an existing discipline code. Bullying is a complex issue that has specific strategies and prevention efforts that should not be addressed as only a discipline issue.

There are several key elements of an effective stand-alone school bullying policy that should be considered (O'Moore, 2000):

- To create a school culture that encourages children to report and discuss incidents of bullying
- To raise awareness of bullying and identify it as an unacceptable behavior with all of the school staff, students, and parents
- To ensure comprehensive monitoring of all areas of school and all school activities
- To establish procedures for noting and reporting incidents of bullying
- To establish procedures for investigating and dealing with incidents of bullying
- To establish support for those affected by bullying behavior and for those involved in bullying
- To work with various local agencies in countering all forms of bullying
- To evaluate the effectiveness of school policy on reducing bullying behavior

It is important to remember that no policy on bullying will be effective if it is not in the context of a bullying prevention program that intervenes simultaneously on all levels of the ecology. It must have a firm commitment from the leadership of the school and district, and the policy should be evaluated regularly.

Develop a Bullying Prevention Committee to Drive Prevention Program

The efforts of a bullying prevention committee will have a dramatic affect on change in school climate and drive the implementation beyond its initial efforts. Typically, intervention begins in this stage in work groups. These groups are dedicated to bringing together various representatives of concerned people to problem solve and devise solutions. Interdisciplinary leaders, or those who have a passion for bullying prevention, should be considered for these work groups. Schools should try to appoint a representative of all employees within the school, including a principal or assistant principal, teachers, and nonteaching staff, such as cafeteria and custodial staff, bus drivers, and the school resource officer. Intervention at this level in the school setting must be seen as a schoolwide intervention.

The coordinating committee generally works with a trained consultant, who trains the committee on bullying prevention and assists in developing a comprehensive bullying prevention program that has interventions at all levels of the school ecology. The committee would then train all the staff and students of the school and ensure ongoing implementation of the bullying prevention interventions.

Train All School Staff

Everyone has their own concept of bullying drawn from a variety of situations: our childhood experiences with bullying, what others have told us as we grew up, and what we have learned in our adult years. Many of our ideas about bullying can come from long-held myths. For this reason, it is important to train all staff on the true nature of bullying, the policy and procedures of the prevention program that will be implemented in the school, and the interventions that will be used within the school setting.

Use Internal and External Experts

It is often helpful to have a consultant assist with any schoolwide transformation. Consultants are recommended because they have expertise in the process of consultation and bullying prevention. They can focus the group to become as effective and efficient in reaching the goals it has created. The consultation process begins typically with an initial discussion between the consultant and someone from the administration of the school. Development of a committee follows, and the consultant guides the group through a process of planning and implementing goals established for school policy and bullying prevention and intervention

Table 2.5   Goals at the Macrolevel

Adapt policy to conform to state and federal law
Use media to announce bullying prevention efforts
Advocate to reduce school violence

strategies. Consultation with a bullying prevention expert increases the likelihood of obtaining one of the essential ingredients of the ecological approach, which is to increase the resources of the school. Having the in-house expertise of a bullying prevention committee meets a second essential ingredient: sustainability. Following the first year of implementation, the consultant serves only as a resource to the school. The bullying prevention committee takes the responsibility for sustaining the enthusiasm and implementation beyond the first year.

Macrosystem

The macrosystem is the context that is the most distant from the individual. The macrosystem includes broader societal attitudes (Barboza et al., 2009), and these attitudes might be influenced by the media and various subcultures. An example of macrosystem influence could be the belief of one's inability to escape poverty based on the cultural beliefs of a community with a low socioeconomic level. Interventions specific to the macrosystem are given in Table 2.5.

Adapt Policy to Conform to State and Federal Law

A transformation that is happening across the country related to bullying prevention is that legislation is now reforming educational approaches, with states enacting antibullying laws. Many states are now providing model policies that can be easily adopted into existing school policy. Schools need to be aware of recent legislation and adapt their school policy accordingly.

Use Media to Announce Bullying Prevention Efforts

The primary macrolevel intervention in the school setting is to use local media to educate the public on the harmful effects of bullying victimization or how they can join in prevention efforts. Schools have found many creative ways to do this, including having the mayor of the city make a proclamation for a bullying prevention day, public service announcements, and offering interviews for local television.

Advocate to Reduce School Violence

Advocacy is another intervention at this level. Brenda High and Robin Todd are examples of how individuals can lead successful advocacy at the macrolevel. They have developed comprehensive Web sites (http://www.jaredstory.com, http://www.bullypolice.org), have written a book on bullying and suicide, and work within their communities to have an impact on bullying prevention legislation. Other media for advocacy efforts can be social networking sites such as Twitter, Facebook, YouTube, and MySpace.

3

INCONSPICUOUS PARTNERS

Bullying as a Precursor to Suicide and Homicide

Every where I go, I am a nameless victim,
Everywhere I hide, they find me once again.
Every time they see me, I put a happy face on,
Every time they leave me, the tears roll down my cheeks.
Every night I'm sleeping, I dream of faceless horrors,
Every day I'm living, I wish it were not so.

Kathleen Kiker[1]

Bullying Is Child Abuse

The poem by Kathleen Kiker, a young person posting her pain on the Writing Circle Web site, shows the desperation of a young person who is experiencing child abuse that inflicts pain on the very core of her being: an all-consuming torment that speaks of an indiscriminate hate, reduction to nothingness, and the longing for escape from the behavior and the pain it causes. The abuse she is experiencing does not fall into the usual understanding of child abuse because the behavior is often seen as typical childhood behavior and even a part of growing up; the perpetrators of this type of abuse are her own age or slightly older and are often not seen as abusers. They are more likely considered individuals unaware of the consequence of their aggressive behavior. Her abuse is bullying.

Most of us in the helping professions are familiar with child abuse because graduate programs spend considerable time training

---

[1] Posting to the Writing Circle Web site (http://circle.nypo.org/kathleen.html) by Kathleen Kiker; retrieved on February 28, 2008.

25

prospective professionals on the ethical standards related to the reporting laws of child abuse and neglect. Determining what is child abuse is another matter. Every state has its own definitions of child abuse that are grounded by federal legislation (federal Child Abuse Prevention and Treatment Act, CAPTA). This legislation defines child abuse and neglect as

- Any recent act or failure to act on the part of a parent or caretaker that results in death, serious physical or emotional harm, sexual abuse or exploitation, or
- An act or failure to act that presents an imminent risk of serious harm (2003, p. 44)

By these definitions, intentionality and harm are key factors in determining child abuse. Intentionality and harm are also present in our understanding and definition of bullying. Generally, the public defines bullying from a broad continuum of teasing, aggression, and even violence. Researchers, on the other hand, are specific that bullying is an unwanted behavior perpetrated by one or more people, that there is an imbalance of power in which the victim has difficulty defending him- or herself, and it is repetitive in nature. There is also intent to cause physical or psychological distress or both. Based on the research definitions of bullying, it is not a broad step to conclude that bulling is a form of child abuse.

The Impact of Bullying

Many years of research have demonstrated that bullying victimization has a significant impact on the health of children who are targeted. The harm caused by bullying can be seen psychologically, socially, physically, emotionally, and academically. Surprisingly, children who bully also have negative consequences, as do those who witness bullying of others.

Schools and Educational Attainment

A recent quotation attributed to a policy maker in Great Britain offers an ecological viewpoint of the broad reach of destruction of school bullying: "Bullying not only scars the life of too many children, it also reflects a serious weakness in our educational system" (Oliver & Candappa, 2003). Certainly, individual characteristics contribute to both being a victim and being a bully, yet we do need to look beyond individual characteristics to consider the context in which the behavior takes place.

High rates of bullying behavior in schools affect the entire school climate. This translates into children not being able to concentrate on learning for a variety of reasons. Children who are potential victims are more fearful of others; children who bully are disrespectful, taking time away from the teacher to address their problematic behavior. Ultimately, children in the school feel insecure and report that they do not like school much. As bullying blossoms in the school, students keenly see that teachers are not responding to stop the bullying, and they view teachers as having no control over what happens.

Victims are more likely to report wanting to avoid attending school and have higher school absenteeism rates (Dake, Price, & Telljohawn, 2003; Rigby, 1996). Students who are frequently bullied by their peers are more likely to report disliking school and receive the lowest grades. Most likely, those children who avoid attending school also miss some of the other benefits of being connected with their school, such as increased mental health, social skill development, problem-solving skills, and resiliency.

Kids who bully also have difficulties with school performance. Their problems center on educational attainment. It would be expected that victims of bullying would show more problems on educational attainment than the kids who bully others because they are more focused on peer relationship problems than concentrating on schoolwork. In fact, being a school bully has more impact on educational attainment than being a victim of bullying. Consider for a moment educational attainment as a student's ability to earn a high school degree. When researchers (Brown & Taylor, 2008) looked at children (15,000 children) born in Great Britain in 1958 and followed them for 42 years, they were able to understand how bullying was related to dropping out of school, obtaining a high school degree, or obtaining a college degree. What they found from their sample was that bullying victimization at age 11 had little effect on whether the person achieved a high school education, yet children who were identified as bullies at age 11 were less likely to have achieved a high school education. However, being a victim has a larger negative impact on wage earnings later in life.

Victims

Bullying victimization has been related to lower self-esteem and higher rates of depression and anxiety. Victimized individuals also have more thoughts of suicide (Dake et al., 2003; Rivers & Noret, 2010). Suicide is certainly a rare event for young people, yet for those who are victimized at the hands of a bully, the risk for suicide increases. Using my data collected from a survey and interviews with 1,900 students (Graham & Losey, 2006), 149 of those students were identified as having a high risk for suicide. An alarming number of the students reported bullying along with suicidal ideation. In the middle school alone, 95 students who engaged in an assessment interview with counselors because they were identified as a suicide risk, 35% (n = 17) indicated that bullying behavior was a significant emotional stressor for them. It is important to note that these students were not asked specifically about bullying incidents.

Why Consider Suicide?

Many people have difficulty understanding why young people would even think about suicide. It is important to consider two possible reasons. In cases of persistent bullying, children may consider suicide as a *means of escaping* from bullying. Children who are relentlessly bullied see no hope for resolving the problem. Their hopelessness is enhanced by irrational thinking, and death seems the only way of removing the despair and pain.

Some young people view their problems as incredibly overwhelming, and they believe even those around them are so affected by the issue that escape for their loved ones would be helpful. In this respect, they see their life as a burden to those they love; for this reason, they believe that choosing suicide will relieve their loved ones, and they will *stop being a burden*.

Table 3.1 Health Consequences of Bullying Victimization

	NOT BULLIED (%)	BULLIED (%)
Headache	6	16
Sleep problems	23	42
Abdominal pain	9	17
Feeling tense	9	20
Anxiety	10	28
Feeling unhappy	6	23
Moderate depression	16	49
Severe depression	2	16

Physical and Emotional Stress

Victims of bullying experience higher rates of mental, emotional, and physical problems. Children who are being bullied have higher risk for headaches, sleeping problems, abdominal pain, anxiety, feeling unhappy, poor appetite, and bed-wetting. Children's depression rates are three to seven times higher when bullied (Fekkes, Pijpers, & Verloove-Vanhorick, 2004). In Table 3.1, it is clear that bullying victimization increases health consequences, and the table identifies the highest disturbances in depression and sleep. Interestingly, sleep disruption has a high correlation with depression. As seen in the table, victims are three times more likely to experience headaches and feel anxious; two times more likely to experience sleep problems, abdominal pains, and feel tense; and eight times more likely to experience severe depression.

Children who experience bullying victimization are also more likely to develop psychotic symptoms. This is particularly true when children experience ongoing, persistent bullying victimization. It has been found that as bullying becomes more chronic or severe, so does the occurrence of psychotic symptoms (Schreier et al., 2009). Consider Michael Carneal, a teenager who attacked a school in Paducah, Kentucky. He maintained that he had psychotic symptoms and may have experienced schizophrenic-type symptoms (according to appeal documents) at the time of the shooting even though he was deemed competent to stand trial. Carneal said that he experienced bullying prior to the shooting. It is possible that the bullying increased his psychotic symptoms.

Lasting Effects of Victimization

The effects of victimization seem to be long lasting. Adults who were former victims of bullying have significantly higher levels of depression, lower levels of self-esteem, and more problems with social isolation, social anxiety, loneliness, worry, and even antisocial behaviors (Olweus, 1993).

Young adults report that they think about their bullying victimization despite being away from the places where the bullying occurred and the people involved. In a survey of college freshmen (Duncan, 1999), approximately half of the students stated that they had been victimized at one time in their childhood, most reporting middle school as the worst grades for victimization, and 46% of these students identified that they continue to think about the bullying victimization.

The consequences for victims of childhood bullying can go beyond even young adulthood. A Danish study of a cohort of men born in 1953 (Lund et al., 2008) suggests that adult men who recall being bullied at school have significantly increased odds of being diagnosed with depression during midlife (ages 31–51) or of having severe depressive symptoms at the age of 51, even after adjustment for social class and parental mental illness.

Bullies

It is not uncommon to hear people describe bullies as individuals who are insecure and possess low self-esteem and who bully others to make themselves feel better. Olweus includes these concepts in his Olweus Bullying Prevention Coordinating training workshop as "common myths of bullying" (Olweus et al., 2005). Olweus believes that bullies actually have little anxiety and insecurity and do not suffer from low self-esteem.

A good number of kids fall into the category of bully-victims, which includes kids who bully others and are victims of bullying. Interestingly, when comparisons are made between pure bullies and bully-victims, bully-victims have significantly lower global self-esteem and harbor significantly more feelings of inadequacy than pure bullies (Kokkinos & Panayiotou, 2004; O'Moore & Kirkham, 2001).

Bullies are more likely to have criminal behavior and legal involvement. Olweus (1989) reported that former school bullies were more likely to have criminal records by age 24. In a longitudinal study in Norway, 60% of boys who were identified as bullies in middle school had at least one conviction by the age of 24, and 35–40% had three or more convictions. Thus, bullies were three to four times as likely as their nonbullying peers to have multiple convictions by their early 20s.

Children who bully others were found to have no consistent association between actively bullying other children and having psychosomatic complaints or depression. However, those children who were being bullied and bullied others were associated with psychosomatic complaints and depression (Fekkes et al., 2004).

There is substantial evidence in the research literature on problems associated with bullying others. Bullying behaviors may be a sign of underlying psychopathology. Kumpulainen and colleagues (2001) found that among bully-victims, oppositional/conduct disorder was twice more common than among bullies and three times more common than among victims. Wolke et al. (2000) noted that bullies have higher rates of hyperactivity and conduct disorder along with lower prosocial behaviors. Austin and Joseph (1996) found more conduct problems for bully-victims than for either bullies only or victims only.

Bystanders

Bystanders are those individuals at school, whether students, teachers, or nonteaching staff, who fail to intervene when bullying is taking place in their presence. Although bystanders do not respond, they are certainly affected by the experience. Bystanders often feel afraid at school and feel powerless to stop the bullying. They may even feel guilty for not taking action or in some cases because they joined in with the bullying. All of this may gradually change school attitudes and norms to be less empathetic for the victims (Olweus et al., 2005) and make it more difficult to eradicate bullying victimization.

4

FACTORS THAT INCREASE RISK FOR VICTIMS OF BULLYING

With the keyboard as his weapon, the bully violated the sanctity of my home and murdered my child just as surely as if he had crawled through a broken window and choked the life from Jeff with his bare hands. It was not a death that was quick and merciful. It was carried out with lies, rumors, and calculated cruelty portioned out day by day.

Debbie Johnston, contributor to the book *Bullycide in America* and mother of Jeffrey Scott Johnston[1]

Suicide that is a consequence of bullying is not one event but the conclusion to a dynamic process between multiple elements with increasing intensity. It would be difficult to consider all the multiple risk factors when examining risk for victims of bullying. For the purpose of this book, it is necessary to limit the discussion to only those factors most relevant to the victims of bullying. It should be noted that there is no foolproof way to predict who will attempt suicide or school violence, but there are factors that increase the likelihood of such an event. For victims of bullying, I discuss the specific factors that increase the likelihood of someone attempting suicide or violence. I organize these factors across five domains, which are outlined in Table 4.1.

---

[1] Johnston, D. (2007).

Table 4.1   Specific Risk Factors for Victims of Bullying

BULLYING	COGNITIVE	MENTAL HEALTH	SOCIAL CONTEXT	FAMILY CONTEXT
Persistence	Interpersonal discord	Mood disorders	Bystander inactivity	Family characteristics
Perceived access	A view of self as a burden	Hopelessness	Belonging	Suicide history
Perceived ability to escape	Intent, motivation, and means	Impulsivity	Alienation	
Fear and anxiety	Negative thoughts	Substance use/ abuse	Recent loss/ rejection	
Victim characteristics				

Bullying

Persistence

Bullying by definition happens repeatedly and occurs over time. If internal and external resources fail for the victim and the bullying persists, it can take a heavy toll. Persistent bullying can be seen as cumulative trauma, and this trauma can last long beyond childhood, culminating in mental health issues in adulthood. Victims of persistent bullying have lower self-esteem and higher rates of depression, loneliness, and anxiety than do children who are not victimized. Maybe more surprising is that persistent bullying can also lead children to experience real physical aliments. When researchers compared victimized children with those who were not, bullied children were nearly three times as likely to have headaches, two times as likely to have problems sleeping and abdominal pain, and five times as likely to feel unhappy (Fekkes et al., 2004).

Is there a type of bullying that is more associated with suicide? It is logical to believe that physical bullying (pushing, hitting) would be more distressing to children because it seems more dangerous and is viewed as more violent, yet when considering mental health as an indicator of distress, both suicidal ideation and depression appear to be more common among children experiencing indirect bullying, such as being ignored or excluded (Van der Wal, de Wit, & Hirasing, 2003).

Thinking back to the Harry Harlow (1958) experiments from the 1950s, his experiments demonstrate the importance of connectedness with others and the profound choices monkeys and other primates such as humans make when they are isolated from others. Harlow gave young rhesus monkeys a choice between two different "mothers." One was made of soft terrycloth but provided no food. The other was made of wire but provided food from an attached baby bottle. The experiment showed that the baby monkeys spent more time with their cloth mother than with their wire mother, in other words, forsaking food in favor of a furry connection. Harlow's experiment showed the power of social connection. The destructive results of exclusion can also be seen in children who are the victims of bullying.

An example can also be drawn from the behavior of Japanese children who bully. Bullying, called *ijime* in Japanese, takes on an extreme nature when Japanese children shun others. Shunning in American culture refers to bullying that is done by social isolation or leaving other children out on purpose, typically to hurt the feelings of the victim or to control their participation in a social activity. In Japan, shunning is the exclusion of a peer through ignoring; typically, shunning takes place when someone is slightly different from the group. In Japan, shunning is not just ignoring, however, because students who use this form of bullying act as if the victim does not exist (Tanaka, 2001). The most troublesome feature in Japanese shunning is the collective nature of it. Shunned Japanese children are treated as nonexistent by the entire class or grade.

Shunning that persists for a long time can be seen as cumulative trauma. The negative effects of bullying build over time and can last well into adulthood. Children victimized by shunning can have a severe distortion or loss of identity. The cumulative trauma of shunning can lead children to believe that they will be permanently rejected by others and to see themselves as lacking the ability to successfully protect themselves in seemingly all situations (Van der Wal et al., 2003). With shunning the most common form of bullying in Japan, with almost 57% of Japanese children saying that they have experienced shunning, it should be no surprise then that Japanese have overall higher prevalence rates of suicide completion than American children (Bridge, Goldstein, & Brent, 2006).

Perceived Access

Our digital age provides many media for communication. Any parent can tell you that peer connection through social media among teens and even younger children is pervasive. Children get up in the morning and check their e-mail, text friends on the way to school, and use the Internet for class assignments. They communicate using Facebook, and they post blogs; all the while, they are twittering their every movement to anyone who wants to be considered a friend. For the child who is being bullied, it may feel as an insurmountable task to avoid the insults and injury that grab the attention of others in the cyberworld. Parents sometimes tell me that children should be able to turn all the electronics off and ultimately stop the bullying. The problem with that perspective is that the majority of their classmates are continuing to connect with social media, along with potentially 100,000 other people in the world, and their classmates will be retuning to school the next day talking about the most recent social news.

For the person being bullied and harassed using social media, hope will diminish if they believe the harasser has a high level of access to their private and social world. Perceptions of elevated access and an inability to escape will require a level of coping strategies that young people may not possess.

Perceived Ability to Escape

When Desire´ Dreyer returned home from school around 3:30 p.m. each school day, she had yet to endure the tempest of rumors and threats that would be transmitted through text and phone messages. Some days, Desire´ would receive text messages on her cell phone from several different girls every 10 minutes until late in the evening. Some evenings, text messages would be combined with threatening phone calls. Eventually, the sound of a phone call or the vibration of her cell phone created a great emotional reaction that manifested itself in depression, anxiety, self-hatred, and suicidal thinking. Turning off the cell phone was not really an option because the messages would be there when she turned it on in the morning before school. She guessed that it would be better to know what they were saying and have the time to react to it instead of "blowing up" after reading them in the morning. For her waking moments, the bullying was ever present, with no possibility of escape, and her nighttime was filled with dreams of fear, revenge, and escape. One day, when the options of escape failed her, suicide became the viable option, and she explored it with ferocity.

Fear and Anxiety

Fear and anxiety can be considered both a *contributing* factor of bullying victimization and also a *consequence*. They contribute to victimization because when a child feels fearful and anxious, the fear can indicate to other students that the child is an easy target. From this perspective, the child is more likely to be victimized. They are a consequence because children who have been traumatized by bullying tend to feel embarrassed and inadequate to handle the situation. Without the understanding of how to stop the bullying through the use of personal skills or seeking help, their fear and anxiety increase as they consider the possibility that they will encounter another situation in which they cannot control.

Fear and anxiety are significant factors that increase the likelihood that bullying victimization will occur in the future. Children will need to understand how to manage fear and anxiety during situations of bullying and understand how expressing feelings during bullying impact the outcome.

Victim Characteristics

Victims are chosen because of the individual characteristics they possess that somehow let others know that they are timid, reactionary, or unwilling to stand up for themselves. There are two main types of victims: the "passive" victim and the "provocative" victim. The passive victim is probably how most people view bullying victimization. Passive victims are quiet, cautious, and sensitive and have little self-confidence. The boys are usually physically weaker than their peers, and the girls are often those who physically mature earlier than their peers.

Provocative victims, on the other hand, actually contribute to their own victimization. Initially, it may sound odd to suggest that children would actually provoke others to bully them. This does not mean that they want to be victimized. However, their behavior does have a provoking essence that irritates others (Solberg, Olweus, & Endresen, 2007). Since the provocative victim is likely to have difficulty reading social signals, the victim continues the provoking behavior, increasing the likelihood that others will be aggressive toward them. In addition, the victim attempts to fight back when feeling attacked or insulted; this increases the probability of victimization because children who bully may enjoy seeing the victim lose his or her temper.

Years ago, I worked in a middle school as a group leader in a self-contained classroom for children with behavior problems. One boy in particular, Nick, had a peculiarity in that he believed he could speak Vulcan, the language of the science officer Spock on *Star Trek*. After some time in the class, I also believed that he could speak Vulcan. As Nick spoke about *Star Trek*, he somehow missed the looks of disdain and poorly disguised whispering from the other kids in the class and inaccurately judged the social inappropriateness of his behavior. So, most kids in the classroom, and a few teachers in the school, were easily irritated by Nick. The children would challenge him, tease him, and with little effort were able to get him to become angry and lash out at others. This usually led to Nick getting into trouble with a teacher, who was already annoyed because of his continued interruptions to the class.

Cognitive

Interpersonal Discord

The most common precipitants for adolescent suicidal behavior are interpersonal conflict or loss, particularly for youth with substance abuse issues. The more unyielding the discord, the more likely a suicide attempter is to have repeat attempts (Bridge et al., 2006). Interpersonal discord can result from peer relationship issues due to bullying by others or from conflictual relationships in a student's family. There is a connection between bullying victimization and family discord; children who experience family discord experience more bullying victimization. Suicide risk increases with the combination of these factors.

A View of Self as a Burden

Sitting in the library at a local school, I listened as a grieving student remarked that suicide is the most selfish thing a person could do. The day before, her classmate had completed suicide, and I was part of a community response team providing crisis counseling at the school. On the surface, her comment struck me as an accurate statement. The teenager's logic was based on her understanding of the considerable hurt she was experiencing and the devastating crisis befallen on family members, friends, and acquaintances; therefore, she concluded that her friend was only thinking of herself. I have heard another perspective as well from a young boy who was considering suicide; he said that he wanted to escape his own torment, and he mused that if he committed suicide he would also have the added bonus of relieving the burden for his parents, a notion that had a stronger presence in his thinking over time. Obviously, this is a distorted perception, yet perceiving that one is a burden to loved ones is a predictor of suicide. Thomas Joiner (2007), the author of the book *Why People Die by Suicide*, believes that this burdensomeness—a feeling of ineffectiveness to the degree that others are burdened by them—is the strongest of all sources for the desire for suicide. Coupled with a feeling of loss of belongingness, this creates a strong potential for suicide.

Intent, Motivation, and Means

Suicidal intent is the extent to which the suicidal person wishes to die. It is a strong predictive factor for repeated suicide attempts and completed suicide. Suicide intent has four features: (a) belief about the intent; (b) preparation before the attempt; (c) prevention of discovery; and (d) communication (Bridge et al., 2006). Students who have the highest levels of intent are those who express a strong wish to die, they indicate evidence of planning, their timing indicates a strategy to avoid detection, and they communicate the intent of their suicide ahead of time.

Motivation is the reason that a person chooses to commit suicide. For teens with the highest suicidal intent, their motivation is to die or to escape a psychologically painful situation permanently (Kienhorst,

De Wilde, Diekstra, & Wolters, 1995). In the context of bullying, the level of the desire to escape is clearly relevant.

It is logical to think that people who attempt suicide and live may not have the same strength of intent as someone who completes suicide. In actuality, there are many factors that influence the outcome of an attempt, such as the availability and acceptability of method and the attempters' knowledge of the likely lethality of a given method. An attempter may choose a method based on the availably of the lethal agent in the home, based on whether it hurts, or based on their belief of its lethality. Many people who attempt suicide have inflated expectations about the lethality of common methods (Harvard School of Public Health, 2010) and may choose a method misbelieving it to be lethal. Therefore, means is a critical factor for suicide risk independent of the attempter characteristics.

Negative Thoughts

The central concept here is that suicidal ideation lies on a continuum of progressing levels of negative thought going from self-depreciating thoughts to thoughts that are obsessive and action oriented and challenge the person to harm him- or herself. The three categories of the continuum are outlined in Table 4.2.

In the first level, the person begins to have less value for him- or herself and has cynical attitudes toward others. They have thoughts that support and encourage isolation and quitting pleasurable activities. When they do isolate themselves, they have more negative thoughts, such as self-contempt and self-abusive attitudes. It becomes a building cycle of increasing isolation that leads to increasing negative thought.

For the second level, the person thinks that using substances such as alcohol or marijuana may help him or her cope with problems.

Table 4.2   Continuum of Negative Thought

Thoughts that lead to lower self-esteem and encourage inwardness
Thoughts that support and drive the cycle of addictions
Thoughts that lead to suicide

Source: Adapted from Firestone and Catlett, 2009.

At first, the alcohol, for example, seems to work to relieve the stress of the presenting problem. Soon, the same amount of alcohol is not enough because the person has developed a physical dependence on it. Since the brain seeks to replicate pleasurable experiences and the person's thinking is increasingly focused on escaping pain, the person increases the amount of alcohol consumed to achieve the same level of relieving effect. This can be the beginning of the cycle of addiction. If addiction does occur, the person will continue a pattern of increasing use despite the negative consequences experienced. The danger for suicide increases with any use of alcohol and drugs; this is because substances weaken inhibition and rationality and increase the possibility that the person will act in an impulsive manner.

In the third level, thoughts are of hopelessness, and the thoughts support withdrawing from family and friends and giving up their favorite activities. They begin to think of death and inflicting self-harm and strategize the details of suicide in a practical manner. Thoughts of suicide at this point are often obsessive and all consuming and challenge the person to commit suicide.

Mental Health

Mood Disorders

Although any psychiatric disorder increases the risk of suicide, mood disorders contribute substantially to both attempted and completed suicides. Although it is true that most depressed people are not suicidal, most suicidal people are depressed ("Act Now to Stop a Suicide," 2010). Research has shown that more than 90% of people who commit suicide had depression or another diagnosable mental or substance abuse disorder (Guo & Harstall, 2004). The World Health Organization, in a study of suicides across several countries, actually found that 98% of individuals who completed suicide had some form of mental health disorder (Bertolote & Fleischmann, 2010). Studies from Sweden, Hungary, Denmark, Western Samoa, the United Kingdom, the United States, and Australia were reviewed. Of the 5,588 people who committed suicide in the collective research, it is evident that only 2% had no indication of a mental disorder at the

Table 4.3 Depression Rates for Bullied Children

DEPRESSION SCALE	NOT BULLIED (%)	BULLIED (%)
Moderate indication	16	49
Strong indication	2	16

time of death. The disorders delineated that 24% of the people had mood disorders, 22% had neurotic and personality disorders, 18% abused alcohol and other drugs, 10% had schizophrenia, 5% had organic brain syndromes, and 21% had other mental disorders.

When comparing victims and nonvictims of bullying, we see a definitive difference in depression rates in children. As seen in Table 4.3, when children indicate that they are depressed, bullied children are three times as likely to report moderate indication of depression and eight times more likely to report a strong indication of depression (Fekkes et al., 2004).

Hopelessness

Hopelessness is a pattern of thinking in which students are unable to see things getting better in the future. The curious thing is that hopelessness is a feature of depression, yet hopelessness is a pattern of thinking that fuels depression. The expression of hopelessness in combination with a mental disorder such as depression represents a serious warning sign for suicide.

Impulsivity

Many therapists will tell teens that suicide is a permanent solution to a temporary problem. A young person who is depressed and is ruminating in negative thoughts may begin to explore and practice the method of suicide. This may go on for a fairly long period of time. As the individual practices, he or she gathers the materials needed and identifies the location and the process or method to use. The young person becomes "practiced" in his or her suicide. Then, when a situation occurs that results in an intense emotional reaction (e.g., the break up of a relationship by a girlfriend or the death of a loved one), the youth is prepared to take a well-rehearsed suicide plan and put it into place with lethal consequence.

Dennis, a school administrator, shared with me the circumstances of a local school principal who days earlier leapt to her death from one of the tallest bridges over a gorge in northern Cincinnati, Ohio. He described the horror of a truck driver who had observed an erratically driven car that then stopped abruptly in the middle of the bridge. The trucker assumed that the person was having car trouble, slowed to offer help, and witnessed the driver rush from her car and, assumingly without thought, run to the edge of the bridge and jump from the barrier to disappear from sight.

Her act of escape through suicide was surely impulsive because it was enveloped in a moment of intense emotion. Although impulsive, the patchwork for lethality was laid by the progressive development of an articulated plan that included frequent thoughts about the suicide prior to the act, planning and rehearsal to some degree over time, and daily rumination about the possibilities of escape through suicide. As evidence for that premise, weeks earlier Dennis heard her whimsically ask, "What would it be like if someone jumped off that bridge?" as they drove past it when returning from an out-of-town meeting.

Substance Use and Abuse

Research has connected substance use with an increased risk of suicide among children. The National Household Survey on Drug Abuse found that children who reported alcohol or illicit drug use were three times more likely than those who did not use illicit drugs to be at risk for suicide (Office of Applied Studies, 2002). When young people become addicted, it raises the risk for suicide, even in the absence of a mood disorder, such as major depression.

When students use alcohol and drugs, it also increases the likelihood of impulsive behavior. This is a disturbing fact when it is known that students who have suicidal ideation practice and plan their suicide over the course of time. The combination of practice and impulsivity can be deadly.

Social Context

Bystander Inactivity

A policy maker in Great Britain offers an ecological viewpoint of the broad reach of destruction of school bullying; bullying not only scars the life of too many children but also reflects a serious weakness in our educational system (Oliver & Candappa, 2003). Certainly, individual characteristics contribute to both being a victim and being a bully, yet we do need to look beyond individual characteristics to consider the context in which the behavior takes place; this most often is in the school setting.

Multiple factors operate simultaneously to perpetuate bullying in the social context. Victims are selected by bullies because of their anxious or passive behavior; as a result, victims are not likely to make assertive efforts to stop the bullying (Limber, Mullin-Rindler, Riese, Flerx, & Snyder, 2004). This also results in a substantial portion of victims who do not tell others about being bullied. Bullies are uninterested in giving up their behavior because of the social rewards they get from bullying.

The majority of the children in the social context are neither bullies nor victims but bystanders who are in close proximity to the bullying. Unfortunately, the majority of the students who are bystanders to the bullying do nothing to help the victim. Paradoxically, some of those children want to intervene but are too reluctant to do so.

When fourth- to sixth-grade students in South Carolina (Limber et al., 2004) were asked what they usually do when they see a student being bullied, they responded as outlined in Figure 4.1.

A full 65% of the students indicated that they would do nothing if they witnessed bullying (38% said that they do nothing because it is

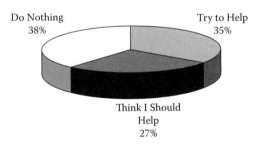

Figure 4.1 Children's helping behavior.

none of their business, and 27% said they do nothing but think they should help). Plus, 35% said that they would try to help the victim. An important message that can be taken from these data is that there are a good number of children who want to intervene. I would guess that if some of the reasons children choose not to intervene are challenged, more children would do so.

There are many reasons why children do not intervene. My own children, who were all under the age of 13 as I wrote this, have on several occasions told me the cardinal rule of all elementary school-children, a rule that surely has been passed down through the ages of kiddom: You cannot be a tattletale. Kids "know" that if you tell, you could make things much worse and could be attacked by the bully, picked on yourself, or ostracized by classmates for telling. Other children stand back and do nothing because they do not know what to do. Others, having seen this happen repeatedly at the school and maybe even regarding this particular child, develop a sense of apathy for the victim and no longer are appalled by the behavior.

Children also know the power of popularity. When it comes right down to it, children are probably more concerned about their popularity than they are about their academic success. Often, the bully is the popular student, and if a child intervenes against a popular student, the child may hurt his or her own popularity.

Michael Thompson, appearing on an episode of *20/20,* "The In Crowd and Social Cruelty," on ABC with Jon Stossel (2001), stated that when children view a bully's aggressive behavior, 21% of them will imitate the bully's behavior. He believes that identifying with the victim makes children feel weak, while identifying with the bully makes kids feel strong. Again, children place high importance on how they are viewed by their peer group.

It is important to look at what happens when children do intervene. In Canada, researchers observed first- though sixth-grade children on the playground (Hawkins, Pepler, & Craig, 2001), and they found that when bullying incidents occurred, other children were nearby during 88% of the incidents and yet intervened only 19% of the time. In almost half of the incidents, the children who did intervene did it aggressively. Interestingly, half of the interventions were effective in stopping the bullying.

Children are also less likely to intervene when other bystanders are present. Responsibility is diffused, and children run the greater risk of embarrassment if they misinterpret the situation and over-react or misjudge others' responses to their intervention (Stueve et al., 2006).

Belonging

We all strive to belong. The idea that teenagers want to assert their independence through the clothes they wear or the music they listen to is really a misinterpretation. In reality, the clothes they wear or the music they listen to is really an affirmation of the group to which they belong. The need to belong to a group or relationship is a fundamental human desire. When this need is not satisfied, a whole host of negative outcomes on health and well-being occur.

The need to belong is so powerful that, when satisfied, it can prevent suicide even when the person believes he or she is a burden to loved ones and has the ability to carry out lethal self-injury. Likewise, when the need is unsatisfied, the risk for suicide increases (Joiner, 2007).

Alienation

By Bullies and Allies   As I mentioned, bullies are often the popular children. As bullying persists, this is reinforced, and the bullies are increasingly viewed as dominant or gaining some social distinction. Students who normally would object to bullying behavior have a weakening of normal inhibition against the bullying (Limber et al., 2004). This may also lead children to become supporters of or participants in the bullying. If the bullying persists for a particular victim over time, children begin to view the victim in a more negative way and may view the victim as worthless or deserving of the bullying. This has an isolating effect for the child because he or she feels alone to solve the problem of bullying, and it also becomes a greater risk for peers to associate with or support the victim.

By Self via Isolation and Depression   There is a curious reciprocal nature to isolation and depression. As a person becomes depressed, he or she tends to isolate him- or herself more. The isolation serves as a depressing agent in that the person is left alone with negative, self-loathing thoughts and increasingly becomes more depressed. The more time the person has to stew in isolation, the more likely it is that the person will progress through a continuum of negative thoughts that encourage hatred for self and self-harm.

Recent Loss or Rejection

Along with interpersonal discord, loss and rejection are the number one precipitators to suicide. The reason that loss and rejection create the risk of suicide is that they create an intense emotional experience that is sustained over a period of time. Young people, who may not have the skills to deal with these intense emotions, may try to escape the feelings by attempting suicide.

Family Context

Family Characteristics

According to the U.S. Department of Health and Human Services (2008), nearly 80% of those who committed child abuse were parents. Of these parents, more than 90% were the biological parent of the victim. Another 6% were other relatives of the victim. Clearly, child abuse is a family issue.

Children learn to navigate their world from what they learn from their parents and siblings. For children growing up in violent or aggressive families, some of their interactions may appear to be adaptive strategies within their family context, for example, a child's "hyperawareness" to potential threats by others as a result of living in an unpredictable, hostile environment. These same interactions are fairly problematic when the child interacts with others outside the family.

John Dussich (Dussich & Maekoya, 2007), from California State University, suggests that children who are physically abused learn that there are two basic relationship types. First, there are power relationships in which one person tries to dominate others. These individuals tend to express anger and aggression. Second, there are vulnerable relationships, in which there is loneliness, isolation, and powerlessness. For the children who have categorized their family relationships on the basis of "victims and victimizers," it becomes easy to translate this to their relationship with peers and other nonviolent relationships (Wolfe, Crooks, & Jaffe, 2009). Too often, these children become the bully-victims, at times using bullying behavior and at other times becoming victims of the aggressive behavior of others.

In a three-country study of children who experienced physical harm, 71% of the children were involved in bullying behaviors as victims, offenders, or bully-victims (bully-victims are those children who both engage in bullying behaviors and tend to be victimized by others). The majority, however, were bully-victims, which supports Dussich's (Dussich & Maekoya, 2007) view that physically abused children take on characteristics of bully-victims.

In turn, victims of bullying are more likely to have experienced physical and psychological mistreatment, particularly by their mothers. They are also more likely to have been pressured or coerced into unwanted sexual contact during childhood and more often are victims of sexual assaults before the age of 13 than other children.

It is possible that child abuse or sexual assaults contribute to the development of relational styles that bullies like to target, such as a sense of powerlessness, low self-confidence, and ability to detect if others are trustworthy (Duncan, 1999).

So, what are the differences in the families of children who are involved in bullying/victimization problems? First, we need to recognize that there is a variety of risk factors for bullying, including individual characteristics of victims and bullies; contextual factors, such as peer relationships; and environmental factors, such as the school or community. Here, I would like to talk specifically about family factors and identify six different family characteristics that increase risk for bullying and victimization: (a) emotional support, (b) effective communication, (c) parenting techniques, (d) attending behaviors, (e) depression, and (f) income status.

Emotional Support   Children need the emotional support of their families. Children who have low levels of emotional support and feel that their families are not sympathetic to their feelings are more prone to bullying others (Bowers, Smith, & Binney, 1992). Unfortunately, children who bully also restrict their expression of emotions toward family members and have an ambivalent relationship with their siblings. In addition, they have more negative feeling toward family members than do children who do not bully (Connolly & O'Moore, 2003). The lack of emotional support of parents coupled with the child's own restriction of emotions has a mutual influencing effect of perpetuating bullying/victim problems, indicating the strong influence of the emotions expressed between family members on future bullying.

Effective Communication   In families in which positive and effective communication is lacking, children are more likely to be involved in bully-victim problems in school (Rigby, 1994). It seems that positive and caring communication from parents can bolster self-esteem and help children feel competent when interacting with peers and teachers at school. Modeling of effective communication skills by parents teaches children effective strategies for dealing with difficult situations that may happen at school. Interestingly, problematic family communication patterns influence children differently by gender; for example, poor communication in the family is more related to boys' bullying behavior at school, but for girls, poor communication is related to their victimization at school. When considering race or ethnicity, parental communication is associated with bullying behavior for White, Black, and Hispanic children (Spriggs, Iannotti, Nansel, & Haynie, 2007).

Parenting Techniques   In his book *Bullying at School*, Dan Olweus (1993) named three child-rearing factors that he believed were predictive of bullying and victimization. First, he stated that the basic emotional attitude of the parents was a risk factor for children, and he believed that the primary caregiver's attitude, usually that of the mother, toward boys was important. He proposed that a negative basic attitude that lacked warmth increases the risk for later aggression. A second factor is the parent's tolerance of aggressive behavior in the child and how unclear the parent is in setting limits. He proposed that "too little love and care and too much freedom in childhood" (p. 39) strongly set the stage for future bullying and aggressive behavior.

Later researchers contend that this permissive parenting style is also predictive of children who are victimized (Baldry & Farrington, 2000). A third factor is the amount of what Olweus called "power-assertive" parenting strategies. Parents who use aggressive parenting techniques, use physical punishment, and have violent emotional outbursts are more likely to have children who are aggressive.

Attending Behaviors   Parents and siblings of children who bully others actually reinforce negative behavior by paying attention to or laughing when children bully others while ignoring positive behavior when it is displayed. This leads to an overall family interaction that is hostile and is characterized by frequent attacks by most members of the family (Lober & Tengs, 1986). Since negative behaviors are, in a sense, rewarded at home, these behaviors are replicated in the school setting as a means to control or manipulate others.

Depression   The mental wellness of parents can play a critical role in the development of problematic behavior in children. In particular, depression in mothers has been linked to their children's aggressive behavior (Georgiou, 2008). It may be that depressed mothers respond less to their children, and as mentioned, permissive parenting leads to aggressive behavior in children.

Overall maternal responsiveness is also associated with future victimization. Appropriate maternal responsiveness is when a mother responds to her child's needs while having a warm and accepting relationship with the child. Maternal responsiveness is a protective factor for the child against isolation and exclusion from peer groups. Social exclusion at school is less likely to happen if the child has an accepting relationship with his or her mother. One possible explanation may be that when mothers respond to their children's needs it helps children feel secure, and this increases the children's self-esteem (Georgiou, 2008).

So the father's role is not negated, the father–child role is a protective factor for children's externalizing behavior. Children are less likely to bully others in families with fathers who are engaged in child rearing. Father involvement can be particularly important when mother involvement is low (Flouri & Buchanan, 2003), as in the case of depression.

Income Status   The notion that income status has an influence on bullying victimization could be successfully debated from a variety of different perspectives, whether one believes that people of low economic status experience more bullying and victimization or not. Some researchers do believe, however, that bullying and disruptive behavior occur more in families of low socioeconomic status (Elgar, Craig, Boyce, Morgan, & Vella-Zarb, 2009; Shepherd and Farrington, 1995). Children with disruptive behavior disorders have been linked with families in which child-rearing practices are characterized by lack of parental involvement, inconsistency in parenting strategies, and the use of aggression as a form of discipline. These characteristics are more common in low socioeconomic families (Kronenberger & Meyer, 1996; Pinderhughes, Dodge, Bates, Pettit, & Zelli, 2000).

Suicide History

Individually, if a person has a past attempt of suicide, the person is more likely to attempt again. This also holds true for families. If there is a history of either competed suicides in the family or there have been past attempts, there is an elevated risk for suicide for other members of the family.

5

SCREEN

If we knew each other's secrets, what comfort we would find.

John Churton Collins

In October 2006, I was part of a team of counselors who partici-
pated in the Signs of Suicide (SOS) program that was initiated at a
local school in Cincinnati, Ohio. During one of my first interviews,
a young girl sat across from me describing her ambitious schedule,
which included college preparatory classes, band, clubs, and social
activism projects related to bullying prevention. She also talked
about her comparable stress, suicidal ideation, and a year's worth of
torment at the hands of a few girls who bullied her because she was
in band.

Our counselors saw 149 students that day from a high school and
middle school population of about 1,900 students who were identified
as at risk for suicide. We discovered that an alarming number of the
students reported bullying along with suicidal ideation. In the middle
school alone, of 95 students who engaged in an assessment interview
with counselors, 35% (n = 17) indicated that bullying behavior was a
significant emotional stressor for them (Graham & Losey, 2006). It is
important to note that these students were not asked specifically about
bullying incidents. Suicide is a relatively rare event, yet there seems to
be a link between persistent bullying and suicide. For example, in a
study of Australian schoolchildren, those who reported being bullied
at least once a week were twice as likely as their peers to "wish they
were dead" or admit to having a recurring idea of taking their own life
(Limber et al., 2004).

Bullying Lethality Screening Tool

The Bullying Lethality Screening Tool (Appendix A) is intended to be used for students who are referred because school staff is concerned about the student's mental health because he or she is experiencing ongoing bullying by others. Typically, the students may be referred because of depression, disconnection with the school or classmates, self-harm statements, or threats toward others or directed at the school.

The screening tool is a two-page document intended to be quick and to be used as a guide for a semistructured interview with the student. It is only a screen; in other words, it is meant to give the interviewer a global view of the student on specific dimensions to create a context for understanding risk. The outcome should be to identify the "red flags" for concern and then guide the interviewer to connect the student with future supportive services or to further assessment by a trained clinician.

The screening tool screens for five relevant factors. There are several arrows indicating critical items that require follow-up interview questions and clinical assessment.

Two aspects of the tool were added because of frequent requests by clinicians across the country who have attended my workshops. First is the addition of a scoring chart at the bottom of the tool. Many professionals want a method of quantifying the level of risk. It is structured so that you can add the number of checked items in each column, and that number would indicate the level of risk relative to the other columns. The second aspect concerns documentation. Agency clinicians want to maintain the tool in the client's chart to document that they have assessed and addressed (or are addressing) the issue. School professionals are more reluctant to have this information in the school file, fearing that the document will follow the student through the course of his or her school career.

My intention for the screen was not to have it scored because I wanted to provide a global, pictorial view of the elements critical to risk for the student. Filling in the columns is enough for me to see what level of risk is involved. Since my experience is in community counseling, I favor documentation of the entire process, which includes initial

Table 5.1 Content Areas of the Bullying Lethality
Screening Tool

SECTION	CONTENT AREA
1	The scope and impact of bullying victimization
2	Depression
3	Isolation by self and others
4	Suicidal ideation and planning
5	Threat context and type

referral information, screening, assessment, and interventions that I mediated (screen, assess, mediate).

The tool is organized in five sections. Each section, with the exception of The Scope and Impact of Bullying Victimization, has categories to evaluate as low, medium, and high risk (bullying only has medium and high). There are also five content areas, listed in rows that serve as the clinicians' guide for a semistructured interview. These are outlined in Table 5.1 and discussed more fully in this chapter.

Section 1: The Scope and Impact of Bullying Victimization

Bullying persistence and intensity
Critical item: Critical coping responses
Vulnerability of target
Access to target
Target's perceived opportunity for escape

The assumption in this part of the screening tool is that the student is already considered at risk for bullying because the student is referred to the school counselor or mental health worker for issues related to ongoing bullying. For this reason, the screening tool only indicates moderate-to-high risk for scope and impact of bullying victimization. The bullying section then focuses on five dimensions of the bullying victimization experience and is meant to determine if medium or high risk.

In addition, since the student is beginning the screening process at "mild risk," it would be the expectation that regardless of the outcome of the screening interview, supportive measures would be put into place to keep the student safe, help the student address the bullying behavior, process the emotional distress, or provide any of a variety of other supportive responses.

Bullying Persistence and Intensity

It is hard to decide when one is considered to be experiencing typical bullying versus persistent bullying. In general, persistence means that bullying is happening more days than not over a period of 2 weeks or longer. The more important feature is how a student copes with and responds to the bullying behavior. In general, research has linked persistent bullying to negative outcomes, so a look at the long-term nature of the bullying experience is warranted. Here, the screening tool directs the counselor to look at a continuum of weekly, consistent victimization to daily victimization. When the counselor is determining the intensity of bullying victimization, he or she needs to understand it in terms of the student's perception of risk for emotional and physical harm. An assessment of greater intensity would carry greater risk.

Critical Item: Critical Coping Responses

The nature and definition of bullying presupposes that the behavior is repetitive and occurs over time. Bullying in itself is distressing. Critical coping responses are those responses that are seen by outside observers as highly anxious, avoidant or aggressive, and fearful of significant bodily harm or death. They would likely follow when the student's repeated attempts to resolve the problem fail. Critical coping responses are a strong risk factor for suicide because people who are using these responses are in a "fight-or-flight" mode of operation.

Although critical coping responses have a strong relationship with suicide risk, mild coping responses are also associated with suicide risk. A possible explanation for the relationship between mild coping responses and suicide risk may be found in the understanding that suicidal people interpret relatively harmless events as more catastrophic than do nonsuicidal people (Blaauw, Winkel, & Kerkhof, 2001).

Vulnerability of Target

Vulnerability has at least three components. Students are considered vulnerable targets if (a) they have any recognizable difference that is viewed negatively by their peers or have a difference that is imaginary or created by those who are victimizing them; (b) the identified difference is used to hurt them; and (c) they have limited resiliency and coping responses. An example of vulnerable students are kids experiencing mental health issues, those who have social deficits, or those considered gay because of the way they dress or act, regardless of their sexual orientation. They would be tormented because of the difference, and they would have difficulty responding in assertive and healthy ways. Students who meet the three criteria for vulnerability would be considered high risk.

Access to Target

Access to the target should be considered using several criteria. First, it is important to consider the target's *perception of access*. For the target, the perception weighs more heavily than what may be actually occurring. Second, consider *direct access*. Bullies who have direct access to their target, in comparison to those who have less access to the target, are more likely to use serious bullying tactics; therefore, direct access increases risk. It should be understood that direct access certainly encompasses physical proximity, but use of electronic media could also be considered providing direct access.

Risk increases when bullying occurs in *multiple environments*, such as at school and in the neighborhood. Multiple environments also include media, for example, bullying at school and bullying with text messaging. Last, the target's *ability to block or avoid* the bullying indicates level of risk.

When counselors are screening for access, they should consider access by these four dimensions. High risk would be indicated for a student who believes that the aggressor has considerable access that is direct and occurs in multiple environments or in combination with media and the student has difficulty with blocking or avoiding the bullying behavior.

Target's Perceived Opportunity for Escape

Last, targets of bullying feel less threatened when they believe that there is opportunity for escape compared to targets who feel that it is impossible to escape (Blaauw et al., 2001). Students can be considered to have higher risk when the need for active planning for methods of escape increases and the students are unable to devise successful avoidance or escape strategies.

Section 2: Depression

> Critical item: Depressed mood or agitation
> Sleep disruption
> Loss of energy
> Substance use
> Hopelessness
> Concentration

The Depression section of the screening tool follows the *Diagnostic and Statistical Manual of Mental Disorders, Fourth Edition, Text Revision* (*DSM-IV-TR*; American Psychiatric Association, 2000) criteria for depressive episode, with the exception of not including all the criteria and the inclusion of substance use. However, the screen is not meant to diagnose depression. The first criterion, depressed mood, is also identified as a critical item. If the critical item is selected, it would be important to evaluate the student more closely for major depressive disorder and suicidal ideation. Unless the screener is a licensed professional, the student would move to the assessment level of the Bullying Lethality Identification System and be referred to a licensed clinician. Also, note that for younger children, depressed mood could present more as irritability or anxiety.

One of the highest correlations with depression is sleep disturbance. Sleep problems can come in the form of not sleeping enough, sleeping too much, or having disrupted sleep. As sleep is disrupted, it can also lead to problems in concentration.

Questions concerning substance use are added to this section because of the high rate of substance use and other mental health disorders. Students who frequently use alcohol or other drugs as a coping mechanism are at higher risk for suicide. This is because frequent users are likely to use substances during times of intense emotions, resulting in decisions that are impulsive and poorly thought out.

Section 3: Isolation by Self and Others

Alienation by peers
Self-alienation
Family connectedness

In the third section, alienation by peers screens for the increasing level of weakening inhibition of other students who would respond in prosocial ways on behalf of the bullied student. As students respond with less helping behavior on behalf of the victim, the student experiences more bullying and possibly bullying by other students who would not normally bully others.

A curious paradox pattern with depression is that depression and isolation fuel each other. As students become depressed, they tend to isolate themselves. While they are isolating, they are left alone to ruminate with their negative thoughts, which depress them further. This section looks at the degree to which the students are isolating themselves from their supports.

Family connectedness and communication are factors related to both bullying behavior and bullying victimization. This section looks at the continuum of negative and hostile communication, problematic parenting techniques, and responsiveness of parents to their children's specific needs.

Section 4: Suicidal Ideation and Planning

Critical item: Thoughts of death
Critical item: Concern of adults
Losses
Coping
Sense of purpose
Thinking patterns
Burdensomeness

There are two critical items in this section. Thoughts of death is the first and is included in the clinical criteria for depressive episode in the *DSM-IV-TR* (American Psychiatric Association, 2000). It is relatively common to hear students talk about wondering what it would be like to be dead or to have other thoughts about death. Depression is strongly linked to suicidal ideation and completed suicides. I believe that it is important that both the nature of the thoughts and the degree of depression the person is experiencing are explored. If this is checked, a referral for assessment is warranted.

During this part of the interview, if I indicate this critical item is present, I often use a quick screening measure for depression to help confirm depression: the Physician Health Questionnaire 9 (PHQ-9). Initially made for physicians, this is a quick nine-question screening tool to identify level of depression and has fairly high reliability.

The second critical item is concern of adults that the student is likely going to hurt him- or herself or violently act toward others without intervention. This was initially added because when researchers looked at the conditions surrounding school shooters, they discovered that typically an adult had some serious concern for the student prior to the shooting. Concern for the likelihood of imminent risk of suicidal behavior is included here also.

Recent loss such as a death of a loved one or break up with a boyfriend or girlfriend constitutes risk because these events can provoke high emotional arousal. When a recent loss is accompanied by strong emotion, poor coping, and suicidal thought, I would consider this student to be at high risk for suicidal behavior.

People cope with taxing stressful life situations differently. Some people address stress by problem solving. Others modify their thinking, such as use of denial, to disconnect from the problem or to think differently about their problem. Some people emotionally cope by managing difficult feelings or finding outlets for expressing these feelings. We know that males and females tend to prefer different coping strategies, with males typically preferring problem-solving coping strategies and females preferring emotion-focused coping strategies.

High-risk students would be those who have intense emotion and have difficulty regulating these emotions. They are viewed as immobile in their thinking and have difficulty coming up with alternative solutions to their problems.

Thinking of and planning for future events provide a positive direction for suicide prevention. When a student believes that he or she has a purpose, the student is less likely to want to leave family and friends. The high-risk student is one who has thinking patterns that encourage isolation and withdrawal from others, sees no purpose in his or her life, and has little connection to events or activities that he or she feels have meaning. In fact, this student feels that he or she is a burden to others, and that life for family and friends would be better if he or she were not around.

Section 5: Threat Context and Type

Persistent
Plausible
Preparation
Motivation

When we initially designed the screening tool, Section 5 of the tool assessed student resiliency. This is an important concept that should certainly be considered, and yet I believed there needed to be a stronger representation for screening for threat. Since the assessment tools (discussed in later chapters of this book) are intended to flesh out threat to self and others, it made sense to screen for threat as a means of directing the mental health worker to consider assessment.

The "triple P" of persistence, plausibility, and preparation is a good way to determine the risk of the threat. Persistence considers if the threat lasts longer than the immediate situation. Plausibility considers how credible the threat is. For example, does it have details, is there a method, and is it logical? Preparation speaks to both the developmental nature of a threat, such as leakage (the intentional or unintentional conveyance of the threatener's intent, such as drawings, poems, and comments to others), and the planning that may have taken place (practiced with a weapon, stalked the victim). Motivation for the threat could include intense feelings related to the crisis or the use of drugs or alcohol.

RESILIENCY

Suicide assessment is a complex dance between exploring reasons for living and a desire to die. A combination of risk factors alone cannot be measured to determine an individual's fate. Resiliency must be explored, as well.

Resiliency is the ability to bounce back after stress or trauma, and the ability to react positively to negative situations. Resiliency is evident in individuals who have the ability to take a traumatic life event and turn it into a constructive learning experience. It involves using coping strategies and problem solving skills to work through difficult times.

Assessing suicide risk involves exploring environmental factors that put an individual at risk. Vulnerability to suicidal responses is influenced by an accumulation of factors including: family history, personality factors, substance abuse, exposure to suicide, access to weapons and stressful life events. Positive configurations of these factors confer increased resiliency, whereas negative configurations increase vulnerability.

Given the same set of risk and warning signs in two individuals, where one presents with resiliency factors such as connectedness or positive coping skills and the other does not, the overall status is distinctly different. In other words, absence of resiliency may equate to the most significant sign of risk that is revealed in a clinical interview.

Susan Graham, M.Ed., P.C.
Child Focus, Inc.

A high-risk student is one whose threat lasts beyond the immediate situation; has a detailed, logical plan that has strong potential for follow-through; and has planning behind the threat. The student has leaked comments or violent writings or has concerned others by their behavior.

Next Step: Support or Assessment?

The Bullying Lethality Screening Tool is not enough to make a determination of risk. The reason I say this is that I do not want someone to rely only on the score at the bottom of the tool. You need to utilize your professional judgment. Logically, if following the screening you have scored the student predominantly at medium or high risk or you have general concern for the student, move to the next step in the process, which is assessment. For students who you evaluate as low risk, implement supportive strategies. These strategies are outlined in the Mediate section of the book, Chapter 7.

6

ASSESS

Tomorrow you will find out if you live or die.

Mitchell Johnson
Jonesboro, Arkansas, student and school shooter[1]

Assessing Threats of Suicide

There is a variety of ways to assess suicide risk. In general, professionals use three assessment categories: acronyms, checklist, and formal assessments. I believe that in the school settings where I have worked, checklists have been the most utilized. Acronyms are useful to help remember content for assessment purposes, but mental health workers prefer to have a form that documents their assessment. On the other hand, formal instruments are cost prohibitive for schools because of the cost to purchase the instruments, the cost for additional training, and the cost of hiring staff with higher levels of expertise and certification as often required by formal instruments. Checklists are convenient and inexpensive and have extensive content; they give a concise method for documenting assessment content areas and interventions utilized.

Safety

During suicide assessment, it is critical to make certain that the student is safe. This begins with making sure that the student is never left alone until a determination of risk has been made and potentially even longer than that. Since risk may not be determined early, I make

---

[1] "Killings shock Arkansas town." (1998, March 25). *The Capital*, Annapolis, MD, p. 1.

Table 6.1 Factors of Suicide Intent and Lethality

Communication of suicidal thought
Desire for death
Prevention of detection
Evidence of planning
Lethality of method
Motivation for escape

sure that I am with the student at all times, or I have another adult stay with the student until I am available.

Consultation

Student assessment for suicide risk and lethality should not be done in isolation. Although I know that it is not always possible, it is helpful to have another professional available either in the session or for consultation as the assessment occurs. This helps in making the best clinical judgments and mediation strategies. It is also useful to document that another professional concurs with the conclusions made during the assessment.

People who have suicidal ideation are seriously considering suicide as a viable option for escape of the problems they are experiencing. I believe that it is an effective intervention to agree with the student that suicide is an option, but that it is only one option in a range of options. This will likely reduce resistance from the student and make the student more open to discussing the suicidality and potential alternatives.

It also is important to create an atmosphere of support. It is important for the professional to maintain a nonjudgmental approach to the assessment. The more the student believes that the interviewer is calm, competent, and without judgment, the more likely that the student will disclose his or her private thinking process. This will assist in the assessment of intent and lethality.

The Bullying Lethality Identification System Suicide Assessment

Communication of Suicidal Thought   While reading this section, it might be helpful to follow along with the suicide assessment that is included in Appendix B. The first section of the assessment gives a graphic view of the strength of the intent for suicide. Remember that intent has four main features: communication of the intention for suicide, beliefs about the intent (in this case, desire for death), evidence of planning, and prevention of detection. In the section on strength of intent, the professional is asked to make a clinical judgment about the strength of the intent for suicide.

Students who have an elevated level of intent typically communicate their suicidal intent with others. On this factor of intent, if the student has confided in someone about his or her intent, I would mark the student as high on this factor.

Desire for Death

Next, consider the belief about the intent. How strong is the student's desire for death? Some students have vague thoughts about death, which would place them lower on the continuum. Others have a strong desire to die, putting them higher on the continuum.

One way of viewing the desire for death is to look at the absence of the desire to live. The inability to give one or more examples in each of the following areas implies an increased desire for death (Cutter, 2010), and at least one example of each affirms a residual wish to live:

- reasons for living
- daily satisfactions
- immediate goals
- possible future changes for the better
- interests in former activities

Prevention of Detection

People can hide detection in a couple of different ways. They can choose a location to commit suicide where no one can find them until they have died. They can also choose a method that is fast, such as choosing a gun (fast) instead of pills (slow). As an example, a middle-age man chose to go to a remote area of the woods, lie in a hole covered with a piece of plywood and then shoot himself with a gun. There was little chance for detection.

Evidence of Planning

Evidence of planning is a strong risk factor. Typically, when there are higher levels of intent, there will be more practice and planning. Evidence can come from an interview with the student, interviews conducted with other students, or information from parents. Planning activities include obtaining or attempting to obtain the means, such as a rope, gun, or medication; practicing with the means, such as discussing or locating the setting; or any rehearsal of any part of the plan.

Lethality of Method

Chapter 4 discussed that the lethality of method can be considered separate from the characteristic of the person. Some methods are more lethal than others. Firearms are the most lethal and most common method of suicide in the United States. Suicide attempts with a firearm are usually fatal, while those with other methods are less likely to kill (Harvard School of Public Health, 2010). Firearms, unlike many intentional overdoses, do not give any time for others to detect and interrupt the suicide.

Motivation for Escape

Victims of bullying who consider suicide have a strong motivation for escape. They may want to escape the feeling associated with being bullied, escape to relieve their family and friends from the burden of their life, or escape the constant fear of injury or persecution. Regardless, both the desire for death and the desire for escape are strong indicators for suicide.

The Intent and Lethality section of the assessment also provides space for the professional to document information related to the section. This includes the thoughts or comments made by the student; the plan as described by the student; the professional's assessment of the intent and associated risk; and any suicidal behaviors of the student, including any behavioral changes that are different from the student's normal baseline behavior.

History and Mental Status

The next two categories on the assessment are checklists. The more items checked, the more the indication for risk. Each category concludes with the professional's clinical judgment of overall risk from low to high for that category.

In the History section, it is important to keep in mind that the first two items on the checklist, interpersonal conflict and recent loss, are the two leading indicators of adolescent suicide. Also, current mental health diagnoses increase risk, particularly a mood disorder, although any mental health diagnosis current or past increases risk.

In the Mental Status section, I would like to highlight that the casual use of alcohol or drugs increases risk and regular use greatly increases risk. Remember that even though most depressed people do not commit suicide, most people who commit suicide are depressed. Therefore, since there is indication of suicidal ideation by virtue of you completing this assessment with a student, if depression is checked in this section, understand that indicates increased risk.

Response

The next two sections of the assessment are meant to document the professional's response related to the risk of the current situation. It is also helpful as a reminder of those things that need to be completed for safety planning.

In the Safety Planning section, sections should be marked if they have been completed by the person using the assessment. In my practice, I make sure that I complete each of these categories for the safety plan. For me, it is a checklist of things I need to do, and then I check them off as I have completed them. A detailed discussion of elements of a safety plan is provided in Chapter 7.

Other potential responses are identified in the next section of the assessment. These are typical responses that we use in the settings in which I have worked. I would suggest that the assessment user modify this section to meet the needs of the specific agency or school. Any additional information can be noted in the Notes section.

Assessing Threats of School Violence

The Public View of School Shootings

I picked up a copy of *Newsweek* from the shop in the hotel in Lancaster, Pennsylvania, where I was set to speak at a conference. Lancaster County, as you may recall, was the site of the attack on the one-room Old Order Amish School, where five young children were killed and many more were seriously wounded. I checked into my room and thumbed through the headlines and text of the magazine:[2]

- "Making of a Massacre: Quiet and Disturbed, Cho Seung-Hui Seethed, Then Exploded. His Odyssey"
- "Cho cast himself as an Avenging Angel against the 'Christian Criminals' who have raped and sodomized, humiliated and crucified him."
- "Cho had a life and a story, but he seemed not to share it with anyone, except in dark dreams and a final spasm of killing."
- "[Cho] rebuffed the efforts of teachers and roommates to reach out to him and scared the rest away."
- "[Teacher found Cho] arrogant and obnoxious and so withdrawn that she felt as if she was speaking to a 'hole.'"
- "Cho's progression from lonely boy to mass murderer is full of portents, a modern tragedy that might have been avoided if anyone had been able to see with those deadly eyes."

A week and some days earlier, Cho Seung-Hui attacked the Virginia Polytechnic Institute and State University, killing 32 people and wounding 25 others. The headlines and text in *Newsweek* gave an exaggerated sense of Cho and hid an equally sinister truth that was more benign and commonplace. During childhood, Cho had experienced major depressive disorder and was diagnosed with selective mutism, which is a disorder that causes children to choose not to speak in specific locations. Cho's selective mutism caused him to appear quiet and withdrawn at school, and for that Cho was cruelly bullied by classmates and teachers. The experiences of Cho's childhood, bullying and mental health issues, are not as exciting as

---

2 "The mind of a killer." (2007, April 30).

depicted in the news. Fortunately, bullying and emotional issues are more manageable by screening, assessment, and intervention than trying to understand the character described in the news—an avenging angel who rebuffed the efforts of teachers and roommates who were attempting to reach out to him and in a final spasm of killing, exploded in an odyssey of mass murder.

Managing Threats of Violence

There are two important schools of thought on how to assess threats of violence in school settings. The first looks at the nature of the threat. How real and how much danger does the threat really pose? The second looks at the individual characteristics of the potential perpetrator. The combination of the two approaches creates a comprehensive approach to understanding risk associated with the threat of school violence.

The management of threats needs to begin with having a structure in place for the management of threats. The structure should include a method of assessing the seriousness of the threat and a strategy for managing the response to the threat at the school in coordination with the local community. Since threat management is a challenging and comprehensive task, threats of school violence are best evaluated by a team of professionals who have specific and ongoing training in threat assessment. It would be wise for schools to establish a threat assessment team that would include the school administrator, a counselor or psychologist, a school resource officer (a police officer assigned to the school), a teacher, and if possible, a community police officer. I include the community police officer but know that this is not typically possible when the threat is first evaluated. However, if a threat event has been evaluated on the categories that I outline next and is deemed high risk, the school should work in tandem with local law enforcement to ensure the safety of school staff, students, and the community.

School threat policy should be known by school personnel, students, and parents. The school should have a person who is identified as a "threat management coordinator," and this person is notified immediately when a threat has been reported or when staff becomes

Table 6.2　Components of Threat Assessment

Assessment of individual
    Demographics: Potentiating factors/precipitating factors
    Individual characteristics
    Context
    Behavior
Assessment of threat
    Threat type
    Evaluate seriousness of threat with "triple P"
Overall risk level of threat
Overall contextual support for risk
Risk direction
Response

aware of the threat. The coordinator should have full authority to act immediately regarding the threat and respond accordingly.

The Bullying Lethality Identification System: Threat Assessment

In my experience, most students with suicidal ideation and those who threaten school violence are evaluated by the school psychologist, counselor, or school administrator. In the school setting, time and resources are limited, so a threat assessment needs to be concise and complete. This ensures that the threat will get the immediate attention of the appropriate staff, and immediate action can be taken if warranted. Creating a threat assessment that captures an evaluation of the actual threat, the context of the threatener, and the environment can offer a fairly comprehensive view of the risk. Table 6.2 outlines the components of my threat assessment. As you read this section of the book, it would be helpful to consult the Threat Assessment form (Appendix C) because each section of the threat assessment will follow the discussion in this section.

Assessment of Individual

Demographics: Potentiating Factors/Precipitating Factors　Demographically, professionals need to consider the factors that precede the threat of violence. Two categories of factors are relevant. The first category is potentiating factors. These factors have the potential to increase risk, and they lie in the essence of the threatening individual (potentiating). Potentiating factors increase risk when they are paired with a threat of school violence. One potentiating factor is simply male gender. Males are much more likely to follow through with a threat of violence, particularly a school shooting. Other potentiating factors include any existing mental health disorder, particularly disorders that include depression, such as major depressive disorder, adjustment disorder with depressed mood or bipolar disorder. Another potentiating factor is the tendency for the student to use drugs or alcohol.

The second category is precipitating factors. These factors are connected to the event or circumstance to which the threat is attached. Risk is increased when the student has intense feelings that he or she is unable to manage in an appropriate way. The intensity of emotion remains beyond what might normally be expected by other people in the same situation. In the case of school shootings, approximately 70% of the shooters feel that they have been bullied or persecuted in some way, so victimization should be considered a precipitating factor.

Individual Characteristics   There are many individual, personal characteristics of a threatener that together should raise a red flag of concern in the context of the threat of school violence. One characteristic is the temperament of the threatener. Problem temperament includes narcissism, low tolerance for frustration, lacking of empathy for others, intolerant attitude to others, difficulty managing anger, and resentfulness. Having these attributes of temperament would make it easier to aggress toward others.

Threateners with poor coping responses are likely to act in inappropriate ways and be prone to aggressiveness toward self and others. They may be impulsive. Those who externalize blame (in other words, see others as responsible for their problems) may carry resentment and desire to even the score.

Context   I always tell people that bullying is a contextual phenomenon; likewise, any threat and threatener must be seen in context. Context should be considered for family, school, and peer group. As mentioned in the section about factors that contribute to bullying and victimization, there are several characteristics of families that increase the likelihood for children to bully others and to be victimized by others. Likewise, many of these characteristics are contextual concerns for school violence.

Family Context   A family context that supports potential for violence includes the presence of a problematic parent–child relationship that vacillates in intensity, family relationships that lack emotional warmth and intimacy, and parenting characterized as either permissive or harsh. These parents often have little reaction to the pathological behavior of their children; since the child's behavior is challenging, the parents have given in, and the child appears in charge.

School Context   The environment of the school can have a significant impact on the acceptance or prevention of aggression. Schools that have inadequate discipline or, the opposite, harsh or ridged discipline, numerous cliques, a code of silence among students increase risk for any aggressive behavior. These schools create a sense of fear among students because students perceive that the school personnel are not in charge and are incapable of keeping them safe. Students then are less likely to report any potential perpetrators of school violence in fear of repercussion; therefore, students may be aware of risky behavior but will not report it.

Group Context   One of the most powerful influences in a child's life (I believe the only exception is the family) is the peer group. Problematic peer group affiliation includes peers who are together in an exclusive group that shares extremist or violent beliefs. Other problematic groups would include those that promote and support negative behavior or have a negative influence on the student, including those that support the use of drugs and alcohol.

Behavior   We should remember that the threat that we observe at the school is only one observable behavior. There are many more. The FBI (Federal Bureau of Investigation) Academy talks about the importance of "leakage" as an observable behavior for evaluating risk. *Leakage* is the intentional or unintentional cues to feeling, thoughts, fantasies, attitude, or intentions (Critical Incident Response Group, 2005).

These cues can be seen in their writing or drawing, the Web sites they frequent, or their activities. For example, these could include when a student makes a threat to the school, is observed to be overly focused on guns, and has recently been practicing firing various weapons.

I have always believed that past behavior is a fair indicator of future behavior. For this reason, it is important to explore the possibility that the student has a history of aggression toward self or others. Have past events been only threats, or has this student followed through with threats in the past?

Assessment of Threat

Threat Type   Not all threats are equal. There are essentially four types of threats: direct, indirect, conditional, and veiled.

1. Direct threats have a specific target and are straightforward, clear, and explicit. There is no mistake in the intention, for example, "I am going to shoot Mr. Wilson tomorrow in the lunchroom."
2. Indirect threats are more vague and ambiguous. Key components—plan, intended victim, and motivation—are ambiguous, for example, "I could kill everyone in the class if I wanted to."
3. Conditional threats suggest that some violent act will happen unless specific demands are met.
4. Veiled threats strongly imply but do not threaten violence. Veiled threats leave it up to the potential victim to interpret the threat.

Evaluate Seriousness of Threat With "Triple P"   The triple P (persistence, plausibility, preparation) is my way of thinking of three indicators that describe the seriousness of a threat. If you were to weed out all the other assessment criteria in this assessment and look for fundamental elements, these three would be the mainstay. The persistence speaks to the emotional intensity someone experiences when the threat event takes place. If the intensity of the moment and the threat lives beyond the precipitating event, it should be considered persistent. When considering plausibility, the question becomes how much "realness" is in the threat. A plausible threat is one that is clear, direct, time oriented, and victim focused. For preparation, I am looking for any practicing or planning that has happened prior to the threat. If I assess someone who states that they have followed someone and now "knows where they live," they have met my criteria for preparation.

I was working in a partial hospitalization program that had eight teens in each classroom. There were three classrooms in the building. An older boy named David had a simmering hatred for a younger boy in another classroom. From his perspective, this boy was always irritating others in the building. In this example, the day before the event, one of the students in the building had stolen David's "Walkman" (for younger readers, this is the 1990s equivalent of the iPod). On this day, the Walkman was discovered in the courtyard, ditched behind a bush, slightly damaged, and missing the headphones.

Following lunch, David was observed by one of my colleagues sitting alone; the colleague (Kerry) walked over to sit with him. David was busily whittling a small stick against the sidewalk, crafting what looked like a 3-inch spear. He put it in his pocket as Kerry walked up to talk with him.

David was highly angry because he believed that the younger boy he hated had stolen his Walkman and broke it purposefully. As Kerry talked with him, he made the threat that he would hurt him later and planned to "get him" after school. The stick was for sticking the boy in the back. Several hours later, he was still angry and saying that the boy would "pay the price" for damaging his belonging.

This situation met the triple P criteria. The threat was persistent in its emotional intensity, and the threat itself persisted beyond the initial discovery of the damaged goods. It was plausible, even though the exact threat was indirect, because we knew the method and he had the means (the stick), we knew the potential victim, and we knew when the boy would likely be attacked. The preparation was evident in the carving of the spear.

Overall Risk Level of Threat

Once we have an understanding of the type of threat and we understand the dimensional aspect of the threat, we can make an informed decision on the level of threat that exists on a continuum of low, medium, and high. This is based on the judgment of the professional and on all the information gathered in the previous sections of the threat assessment.

A low level of threat is one for which the basic content of the threat is suggestive that the person will not carry it out. The threat lacks detail and just does not seem possible. You would expect to find inconsistency in the details of the threat, and it may appear vague in its content.

A medium-level threat is likely to be more direct in the content and may suggest that there may be a place and time in the threat, but it definitely does not suggest that there is any detailed plan. It would be expected that there was no practice of the threat prior to the threatening incident.

A high level of threat would contain the triple P of the threat assessment: persistence, plausibility, and preparation. The threat would indicate that plans to injure the other person lasted beyond the incident, the threat is plausible in its content, and the threatener has practiced a plan to injure the potential victim.

In Chapter 7, I discuss these categories and the appropriate interventions that correspond to the level of threat in the mediate process of the Bullying Lethality Identification System (screen, assess, mediate).

Overall Contextual Support for Risk

The section on overall contextual support for risk is also for the professional to make a judgment based on the previous content of the threat assessment. The professional is asked to view each area of the individual characteristics and contextual factors and make an informed decision based on a continuum of low, medium, or high.

Risk Direction

I have included a section to document risk direction. This section is intended to demonstrate that the direction of the threat has been considered. It is important to remember that if any identifiable target or person is indicated, they must be notified of the potential threat. Notification should be documented in the notes section of the threat assessment.

Response

The Response section of the threat assessment is to ensure that the professional documents the response to the threat. There are a multitude of responses that a professional can make, too many to include on this threat assessment. The ones included here are the responses we are most likely to use in our school setting. Your program can change this section to meet the needs of your school or program. Many responses are discussed in further detail in Chapter 7.

7
MEDIATE

Bullying is the foundation on which a lot of subsequent aggressive behavior gets built. If [the rate of school bullying] is going down, we will reap benefits in the future in the form of lower rates of violent crime and spousal assaults.[1]

David Finkelhor

University of New Hampshire, Crimes
Against Children Research Center

I use the term *mediate* when discussing methods of intervening in bullying, suicide, or school violence. I think the term captures the interactive nature of prevention and intervention work with students. To mediate in bullying or suicide, you are not "doing" something to someone but working with the person to address a problem. For threats of school violence, our mediation also includes the interaction among school staff, mental health personnel, and local law enforcement. Obviously, there are times when we increase our control in situations by becoming more directive when the crisis becomes dangerous, but for the most part, I like the use of the term. To mediate, then, is to intervene interactively with students and other professionals to implement solutions related to bullying problems, to create safety for students and the community, and to prevent school violence.

---

[1] Cray, D. (2010, March 4). "U.S. survey finds sharp drop in children's bullying." [Reported through the Associated Press.]

Mediating Bullying

I suggest that there are two types of bullying referrals that come to the school counselor's office, and that responses should be a bit different. The first is an initial referral that indicates that bullying may have taken place or may be occurring. The other referral is that bullying has been identified, it potentially has been occurring over an extend period of time, and it may be associated with possible suicidal ideation or threat to others.

Initial Notification or Observance of Bullying

I believe that once an adult is aware that bullying is occurring, the adult becomes responsible for making others aware of it and stopping it. I think it is a mistake to assume that students have the skills and resources to deal with bullying. From my experience, students are more likely to feel embarrassed, to inaccurately take personal responsibility for the problem, and to be frequently unsure of how to deal with it; as a result, they tell no one.

At the time of the initial referral, school staff should ask about the "who, what, where, and when" of the situation and determine if bullying is actually occurring and to what extent. Typically, this is not all that clear. In situations such as this, it is necessary to increase observation of the victim in a variety of contexts within the school setting. This will help ensure the safety of the victim and give a clearer picture of the student's interaction with others. I would also suggest that the potential bully be observed in his or her interactions with others.

Staff should work with the student to help the student understand the helpful resources or people available at school or in the community. Staff should work collaboratively with the student to develop a plan for telling adults and strategies for dealing with future situations. They should also inform the student's parents.

Regular Consultation With Student   I recommend that several sessions of consultation with the student who is bullied occur. Typically, students are confused about why they are being bullied and internalize blame for the victimization they experience. It would be useful to help the student process feelings related to bullying and use this as an opportunity to teach and enhance social skills.

Ongoing or Persistent Bullying

In our age of litigation, it is important that a school intervene swiftly, with the fullness of their abilities and documenting a sound and appropriate response, when it has knowledge of ongoing and persistent bullying. Parents send their children to school and give great responsibility to the school personnel for keeping their children safe. When schools are sued, it is because the school was perceived to have intervened inadequately to help the victim, it ignored the problem, or the parents were not informed by the school about the extent of the bullying victimization their child suffered.

I believe that there are three things that can increase the safety of the student and at the same time decrease the risk of litigation for the school: Staff should intervene immediately, parents should be notified in all situations, and there should be documentation of the event and subsequent staff response. To assist with this process, I have created a documentation form. It might be helpful as you read this section to follow along with the Documentation of Bullying Intervention form (Appendix D).

Parent Notification

As soon as possible, notify parents of students who are the victim of bullying. Depending on the severity of the situation, this notification could be as simple as a note home that informs the parents that their child has been bullied; for more severe situations, it may be necessary to have the parent come in to meet with the teacher, school counselor, or administrator. Parents of the student who did the bullying should be informed. Regardless of the level of risk determined, the parents of the victim should be notified about the incident that led to the referral to your office, the outcome of your risk screening, and interventions that you have implemented or that you plan to implement. You should also ask the parents for their assistance to ensure the safety of the student and challenge them to identify the specific interventions they

Table 7.1   Sample Goals

	DATE IMPLEMENTED	REVIEW DATE
1. ENSURE SAFETY AT LUNCHTIME		
Objective Mr. Henderson will observe Melissa's interaction with peers.	January 17, 2011	January 21, 2011
Mr. Henderson will check in with Melissa one time during lunch period.	January 17, 2011	January 21, 2011
2. MEGHAN WILL DEVELOP SKILLS TO INCREASE BYSTANDER HELP		
Objective Ms. Harper will teach three skills to Meghan that she can use to increase bystander help.	January 17, 2011	January 21, 2011

will do. Offer to call them at a predetermined time in the future to evaluate your interventions and the safety of the student.

I recommend that you also talk with the other students involved in the situation. If you believe them to be involved in bullying the student, focus on the school policy that was violated and discipline the students accordingly. I would also contact the aggressor's parents and discuss your interventions, consequences, and expectations of future behavior.

It is a good idea to document this communication. It is beneficial if the staff person can document a collaborative effort with a parent in remedying the situation. Included in this would be any plan of action coordinated with a parent and any refusal of the parent to take action.

Create a Plan of Action and Target Dates

Staff should develop an individualized, concrete plan of action that has specific, measurable goals and objectives; the plan includes a target date for implementation and follow-up. It is best if this can be done after consulting with the student and his or her parents. Some possible examples of goals can include the items given in Table 7.1.

Mediation Plan

Teach Structured Social Skills

There are two types of victims, and they require two different kinds of skill development. Most of us view victims of bullying as passive victims. They are shy and nonassertive and, in the case of boys, may be physically weaker. These students need to be taught social skills such as assertiveness, how to express feelings, and how to deal with the aggression of others. An excellent resource that I have used with students in my office is the book *Skillstreaming the Adolescent: New Strategies and Perspectives for Teaching Prosocial Skills* by Arnold P. Goldstein et al. (1980). These skills are easily adapted to fit bullying situations.

Provocative victims make up a smaller proportion of bullying victims. They are referred to as provocative because their behavior often provokes others to bully them; however, this does not mean that they want others to bully them. The provocative victim can be like the passive victim but can also be aggressive toward others. Provocative victims often miss critical social cues from their peers that would indicate others' disdain for their behavior. For this reason, they should first be taught how to recognize these cues by developing social awareness skills and then learning social skills, such as those mentioned in *Skillstreaming the Adolescent* (Goldstein et al., 1980).

Develop In-the-Moment Responses

Teach Assertive Behavior   Children who bully enjoy one thing above all other things when they bully: the emotional reaction of the victim. The more the victim reacts emotionally, it seems the more the bullying increases. Therefore, the main element of assertive behavior as it relates to bullying is to react without emotion.

Consider assertive communication as an emotionless communication that declares that this is what I am, this is what I think and feel, and this is what I want or expect. The statement should be short and clear and then move on with the conversation with little concern for the response. If the response challenges what is desired, restate anything that may be agreed on and restate the goal, for example, "Yes, you are right on that part, and I still want … ."

Body language is an important part of responding without emotion. It is estimated that about 9% of what we communicate to other people is verbal, with 55% nonverbal (gestures, expressions); the remaining communication is paraverbal (tone, volume, and cadence). People will trust paraverbal and nonverbal communication over what we say; therefore, it is critical that the sum of the nonverbal communication matches the assertive communication. The person should be at a normal conversational distance, and eye contact should be maintained, facing the person. Voice should have a factual tone and not an emotional tone, and the emphasis should be on determination to get what you need. It would also help to rehearse the conversation ahead of time if that is possible.

Talk, Walk, and Squawk   An interesting strategy that addresses mean or teasing comments from peers is talk, walk, and squawk (Glew, Rivara, & Feudtner, 2000). The first step is to look at the person and say assertively but calmly, "Leave me alone" or "You don't scare me." Once that is stated, the student should walk away. It is best not to run because it shows fear to the aggressor, and walking may give the student a sense of power. Once removed from the situation, the student should "squawk" to a trusted adult. Bystanders should also tell adults when they see another child being bullied.

The Comeback   Because teasing is the most frequent way children bully and students typically tease using the same themes or names repeatedly, it would be helpful to plan ahead for teasing and use a "comeback," which is a prepared response statement. This gives the student a sense of control over the situation and allows for an easier escape—with some dignity.

My favorite comeback strategy is simple yet often effective; it is the "so" strategy. To pull off this strategy, the student should respond to a teasing statement with "So" or "Whatever." To make the strategy successful, the student needs to abruptly leave the situation without any emotional expression.

An obvious initial strategy is the *assertive* strategy. With this, you just ask the bully to stop: "Stop smacking me on the back of the head; I don't like it." Not all bullies will stop, obviously, but it makes sense to try this first.

The *positive confrontation* strategy begins with making a positive comment about the bully and then confronting the behavior of the bully. For example, "I really like what you said to Melanie yesterday; you are much nicer when you are not teasing people."

There are many other ways to plan for teasing. Students could plan for these situations with rehearsal and role-play. For more strategies, I suggest that you read the article "Strategies for Handling Annoying Bullying and Teasing" by Melissa Johnson (2006) (http://www.instituteforgirlsdevelopment.com).

Activate the Bystander

As I have mentioned, bystanders are reluctant to intervene during incidents of bullying. However, the bystander is the critical element in stopping it. Davis and Davis (2007), in their book *Empowering Bystanders in Bullying Prevention,* identify several strategies that school professionals can use to create a foundation that supports safe bystander involvement.

Davis and Davis (2007) recommend that staff should help students understand that keeping silent only creates greater power for students who are aggressive to others. They do not recommend that students confront the aggressor directly, but that methods that are more indirect are safer and typically more effective. It is important that students tell adults about the bullying they observe. It is equally important that when a student tells an adult of a bullying situation, the adult should protect the student from retaliation.

Teaching skills to bystanders is another helpful strategy that may encourage students to take action. Teaching empathy to bystanders may help more students tell adults about the situations they observe. Teaching specific communication and assertive skills may help with deflecting strategies that could deescalate a potential bullying situation.

Ultimately, it will take an ecological approach with interventions on all levels of the school ecology. When staff intervention is consistent and the school environment opposes and does not support aggressive behavior, children feel safer to intervene when observing or experiencing bullying.

Help Parents Intervene

In my experience with my own children, I have found it difficult to separate myself from the concern, fear, and anger that sometimes come when you discover that your child is being picked on by one or more students at school. The following step-by-step process has been adapted from the work of the U.S. Department of Education and Early Childhood Development (2009); it is helpful in giving a structure for how to talk about bullying with your child. School professionals could discuss these steps with parents so that they are prepared for future situations.

Step 1: *Listen* carefully to your child and show that you are concerned. Support the child by offering empathy for the difficult situation.

Step 2: *Give sensible advice*—do not encourage your child to fight back; this will most likely increase the bullying and put the child at risk for being hurt. Remember that bullying is about an imbalance of power, so fighting back could put the child at risk for being hurt.

Step 3: Assist your child to *develop positive strategies,* including

- Using assertive communication: Say "leave me alone" and calmly walk away
- Avoiding situations or places that might expose the child to further bullying
- Making new friends

Step 4: *Ask* your child questions such as the following to understand if there is a repeated pattern:

- What, where, and when did the incident happen?
- Who was involved on each occasion?
- Did anybody else see it, and if so, who?
- What solutions have been tried so far?
- What are the names of any teachers who are aware of the problem?

Step 5: *Work* with your child's school to solve the problem. Do not just call the school and expect the problem to be solved.

Step 6: *Develop* a plan with the school for dealing with the current situation and future bullying incidents.

Step 7: *Follow up* with the school to see what has been done.

Step 8: If needed, ask for the *school counselor* to become involved to provide ongoing support at the school.

Step 9: Encourage your child to *report any further bullying* incidents to a teacher he or she trusts at the school.

Impact of Resiliency Factors

The Search Institute has completed many years of research related to the developmental assets of children and identified many external or internal assets (http://www.search-institute.org/content/40-developmental-assets-adolescents-ages-12-18#). The bullying research is clear that having specific internal and external assets has a significant impact on reducing future bullying behavior and bullying victimization.

Key to risk reduction is the way in which family members engage with each other. The school professional should consider supporting a positive family culture. This could be accomplished by strategies indicated by the school professional or through a referral to a family counselor. Positive outcomes are likely to come from strengthened positive family communication, increased family connectedness, and family support of the student during stressful times.

A caring school environment can make or break a student's success in school. Research from the Olweus Bullying Prevention Program on utilizing weekly class meetings that allow students to talk about problems and express their feelings has a dosage response to outcomes. In other words, the more time you offer for classroom meetings, the more the students participate in prosocial behaviors and enjoy school.

Students who are considering suicide express difficulty finding meaning in their life or in the future. Helping the student to become involved in meaningful activities and articulating their successes will reduce risk.

Mediating Suicidal Ideation and Behavior

Mobility and Action During Crisis

An important concept in intervention during crisis is the dynamic of mobility and action. I consider *mobility* as the capacity for the student to move in ways needed to address the current issue in a healthy

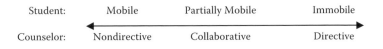

Figure 7.1 Student–counselor dynamic.

manner. Students who can interactively problem solve with the counselor, identify coping strategies for future situations, participate in the assessment process itself, and discuss and implement safety-creating strategies would be considered mobile.

Action refers to the extent the counselor takes control of the developing crisis with a student. The counselor moves on a continuum of nondirective, to collaborative, and to more directive approaches. The student who is fully mobile is relatively autonomous to address situations in his or her life, and for the most part the counselor can take a nondirective approach to the counseling process. As the student becomes more immobile, it is imperative that the counselor take a more directive approach in mediating the situation. This dynamic is illustrated in Figure 7.1.

For the student who is partially mobile, the counselor can collaborate with the client, school, and the student's family to create safety strategies and other interventions to mediate the issues at hand. I focus next on situations in which the students is immobile and the counselor needs to take a directive role in mediating suicide and school violence. This continuum could also be seen in relationship to suicide risk: The more immobile the student is, the higher the level of risk will be.

In many bullying situations, the mediation process following screening and assessment is one of collaboration because the student may have the coping strategies to address the situation yet may need assistance from the counselor in developing strategies to address the issue or for utilizing the discipline system of the school to stop the bullying. Generally, suicidal ideation and threat assessment fall on the left side of the continuum of collaborative-directive.

Before discussing counselor-initiated mediation, I take a moment to recognize peer roles in suicide prevention. Often, peers are silently listening to students conveying their consideration of suicide, and they can make a huge difference in suicide prevention.

Helping Students Mediate

When reviewing the data in our 2003 survey of schools in Clermont County, Ohio, an interesting contradiction became apparent. Students reported that teachers were the most likely to intervene when they told them their concerns about witnessing bullying or being bullied. However, the students were more likely to tell their peers in these situations; unfortunately, they also identified their peers as the least likely to intervene.

In the same sense, students may be talking about suicide to their friends, who may not recognize the signs or symptoms of suicide. Students may not understand that "doing something" is important when a friend confides that he or she is considering suicide. When our team implemented the Signs of Suicide Program in our county, I learned a useful acronym (ACT) that I now teach students so that they know what to do when a friend talks about death or suicide.

The acronym stands for acknowledge, care, and tell (ACT; 2010). Students are told that when someone talks about suicide or hurting him- or herself, they should acknowledge that this is a serious issue and be willing to listen. The friend is more likely to seek help if someone is willing to listen. The student should care for a friend by voicing concern and telling the friend that he or she understands. Caring also includes asking the tough questions, such as asking if there is a plan for committing suicide and how far along the friend is in carrying out the plan. Last, the student needs to tell, and telling means getting professional help immediately. Take the friend to a teacher, school counselor, or mental health counselor at the school. If the friend is in therapy already, immediately get in contact with the therapist. If the friend refuses help, is in immediate danger, and no adults are available to assist, call the police or 911 immediately.

General Guidelines for Mediating Suicide Based on Level of Risk

Paul and Darcy Granello (2008) identify four levels of suicide risk: (a) low, (b) moderate, (c) high, and (d) suicide emergency. Suicide emergency is when the student expresses a clear indication that he or she will commit suicide when the opportunity first presents itself. The

Granellos believe that counselors should generally approach all situations of suicide risk as a suicide emergency until the counselor can prove otherwise.

Mediating low-level risk is indicated when there is no specific or concrete plan. It is important at this level to have ongoing assessment with the student and intense follow-up strategies in place. A risk management or safety plan should also be in place. Counseling should focus on treating the underlying disorder.

Mediating moderate risk is indicated when the student is experiencing suicidal ideation and has a general plan for suicide. Again, ongoing assessment is important at this level, particularly to determine the appropriate level of care. Outpatient therapy is possible when there are appropriate safety strategies in place and there is a supportive home environment.

Mediating high risk is indicated when there is frequent, high-intensity suicidal ideation and a specific and lethal plan with access to means. At this level of risk, an evaluation is necessary to consider if hospitalization is warranted.

Develop and Implement a Treatment Plan

Developing and implementing a treatment plan is critical with suicidal students. It helps provide the best clinical care. It also provides the necessary documentation to reduce liability in a malpractice suit. There are a variety of components essential to providing treatment for students who are at risk for suicide. Table 7.2 presents an overview of recommended components of an outpatient treatment plan (Granello & Granello, 2008).

No-Suicide Contracts

No-suicide contracts are agreements between the counselor and the student intended to obtain a commitment from the student to not commit or attempt suicide. There has always been a debate during my career concerning the usefulness of no-suicide contracts. Some people believe that no-suicide contracts are an important safety strategy, others view them as an intermediary strategy, and others believe that they

Table 7.2 Components of an Outpatient Treatment Plan

Diagnosis	Diagnosis of your client. This speaks to the underlying problem that you are treating. Chart your progress.
Determine need for hospitalization	Ongoing, regular assessment of your client's level of functioning and need for hospitalization or other more restrictive interventions.
Psychiatric evaluation and medication	Consider having a psychiatric evaluation and the possible use of medicine to assist therapy.
Strength of therapeutic relationship	Assess the strength of the therapeutic relationship. If strained, consider referring to another clinician. The relationship is critical to success of treatment.
Ongoing counseling	Consider counseling for a variety of modalities, such as individual, family, group, and support. Consider increasing the number of times that you meet with the client. Telephone to check in with the client.
Consultation and supervision	Regularly seek consultation and supervision. Make sure to document recommendations and follow through with selected interventions.
Education	Educate the client and the client's family to help them manage crisis.

are not worth the paper on which they were written. Even though the debate existed at the agencies and schools where I have worked, it was always required as part of the assessment process, so we did them.

There is a variety of problems with no-harm contracts (McGlothlin, 2007). First, there is little empirical evidence that they actually work. There are only a few research studies in the literature on no-suicide contracts, and in those, there is little evidence that no-suicide contracts keep people from committing suicide. However, clinicians use them, believing that they do deter suicidal behavior, leading clinicians to a dangerous false sense of security. Parenthetically, there is also a fair amount of opposition by the researchers for the role of no-suicide contracts in clinical practice (McMyler & Pryjmachuk, 2008).

Second, counselors generally have no formal training on no-harm contracts. So, they use the no-suicide contract with which they are familiar or they have obtained from a peer and conduct the session in the fashion that they see fit. Last, counselors also fear lawsuits related to suicide and believe that executing the no-harm contract will keep them from being sued. Since no-harm contracts are crafted by mental health professionals and not worded in legal terms, realistically they have little weight in court.

It is true that there can be therapeutic benefits of using no-suicide contracts (develops alliance with student, following the contract can be part of a treatment plan), but a fair amount of caution needs to be exercised to limit the potential dangers. Jason McGlothlin (2007) from Kent State University (Kent, OH) recommends that if no-suicide contracts are used, they should be used only when the counselor believes the client is not in immediate danger. From my experience, this seems contradictory to how I have seen many people use them in practice: The counselor uses the no-suicide contract following a suicide assessment (which has indicated risk) and immediately prior to releasing the student to his or her parent. The hope is that the no-suicide contract will add an extra layer of protection between sessions.

Douglas Jacobs (1999), associate professor from Harvard Medical School (Cambridge, MA) suggested several guidelines for clinicians who use no-suicide contracts. He recommended that contracts should only be used after the therapeutic relationship has been established, should only be used as part of a thorough suicide assessment and treatment plan, should be used with caution and sound clinical judgment, and that clinicians need to remember that when a student signs a contract it does not mean that there is no suicide risk.

Develop a Safety Plan

A safety plan is not the same as a no-harm contract, although I suspect that some people view them as the same. No-harm contracts obtain a commitment from the student that the student will do certain things and agree not to harm themselves; the safety plan is a collaboratively written document that has several components to help the student know the steps to take when things change for the worse and risk for suicide increases. Safety plans are essential for all potentially suicidal students.

There are eight components that I recommend to be included in a safety plan (Table 7.3). These components are adapted from the work of Paul and Darcy Granello (2008) of The Ohio State University (Columbus, OH) and the *Safety Plan Treatment Manual to Reduce Suicide Risk* (Stanley & Brown, 2008) from the Department of Veterans Affairs.

Table 7.3   Components of a Safety Plan

Recognize and avert the potential crisis
Engage social networks
Use internal coping strategies
Avoid risky situations
Utilize positive support when troubled
Continue treatment
Create a safe environment
Know who to call

Recognize and Avert the Potential Crisis   It is important for the student first to recognize the warning signs when they are moving into crisis mode. These warning signs can include specific situations that are particularly distressing, as well as thoughts, images, thinking, mood, or behavior. Once the student is able to recognize the onset of these warning signs, the student can be effective in averting a suicidal crisis before it can fully emerge.

Engage Social Networks   Obtain a commitment from the student to attend social groups that are positive. The expectations would be that they attend healthy social situations, such as going to a coffee shop with friends, attend a church group activity, or become part of a sports activity, such as volleyball once a week. During these events, the goal is to be with people who can offer social support and that the student interact in this setting without discussing his or her suicide thoughts with others.

Use Internal Coping Strategies   Help the student identify a list of activities that they could do without needing to contact other people. These activities can be a way to help students take their minds off their problems and prevent suicidal ideation from escalating. It will be important that the student work with the counselor to strategize these activities to increase the likelihood that the student will actually use them. The specific strategies may or may not include skills that were learned during therapy. For example, students could be taught to use a strategy of positive self-talk and utilize this strategy whenever possible to disrupt negative and suicidal thoughts. However, they may choose to exercise to distract themselves from their negative thinking. The goal here is that the student tries to cope on his or her own with suicidal feelings, even if it is just for a brief time.

Avoid Risky Situations   Help the student see that they can create situations that increase risk, and alternately, the student can reduce risk. During safety planning, encourage the student to identify risky situations and strategies and what they will do to avoid these situations.

An example of a risky situation is activities that increase the opportunity for impulsivity. The student should be encouraged to avoid situations or activities that increase impulsivity. Alcohol and drug use reduces inhibitions and increases the likelihood that a person will act impulsively; therefore, the student should be asked to commit to discontinuing use of drugs and alcohol. Another risky situation is activities that create high emotional intensity, such as seeing an old boyfriend or girlfriend, situations that are frustrating or angering, and spending too much time alone.

Utilize Positive Support When Troubled   Have the student connect with people when life gets difficult. Ask the student to commit to calling or connecting with supportive people when they get bad news or experience stressful situations. Help the student to identify the people in his or her life, typically family and friends, who can offer this support. These people can be those who help distract the student from his or her thoughts, or they could be people who actually help the student manage the suicidal crisis. These people should be identified on the safety plan; their telephone numbers should be included.

Continue Treatment   The student is asked to keep all appointments with doctors, counselors, and other mental health providers. The student is also asked to take all medications as prescribed by a physician. If necessary, the student should consider refilling medication more frequently to have only small amounts on hand.

Create a Safe Environment   Risk for suicide increases when there is an availability of means. It will be important for the safety plan to include the strategy of eliminating or limiting access to potentially lethal means. Examples of this include removing all firearms from the home or keeping them locked and unloaded (preferably given to a trusted friend or even law enforcement) and limiting access to large quantities of medication or potential poisons.

Know Who to Call If the previous strategies are not effective, students should be instructed to call identified professionals or 911 in suicidal emergencies. The safety plan should include the name and phone number of these professionals and how they can be reached or what to do during nonbusiness hours. Suggested contacts include the community crisis hotline, doctor or counselor, case manager, clergy, or family or friend.

Parent Mediating Strategies

When I talk with parents of students who I have assessed for suicidal thoughts or behavior, I ask the parents to be partners in keeping their child safe. I review the warning signs and help predict what they might see if their child moves toward a crisis. Since I have already helped the student recognize the potential crisis in the safety plan, this is fairly easy to share with the parents. I review the safety plan and ask them what parts of it they can help with implementing. I emphasize their responsibility in restricting means and making sure that they know who the "go to" people are in the safety plan.

I also discuss what they can do to maintain healthy communication with their child. For example, I mention the importance of maintaining open and direct dialogue about suicide. I ask them to help their child express his or her feelings, to be accepting of those feelings, and to offer empathy for their child's situation. I tell them to make sure to offer the child hope and to share possible alternatives to suicide and the child's problems.

When the parent or child recognizes that the child is moving in the direction of crisis, parents should help the child use the safety plan. When in doubt, act. Call one of the professionals on the safety plan and make sure that the child is safe until the child can be seen by someone who can determine risk.

Mediating Threats to Others or of School Violence

School Policy

The foundation of addressing school violence is the local school policy. Although it is not within the scope of this book to detail school policy, let us briefly discuss some of the components of a violence-free school policy (Ontario Ministry of Education, 2008). This is not all inclusive but does address some of the main categories to be considered.

> *School environment:* It is important to consider the school environment as both the physical and social environment. Here, the policy should focus on achieving a safe school by securing unsafe areas, maintaining the presence of responsible adults in school areas, and addressing visitors and strangers in the school.
>
> *Curriculum-based violence prevention*: Violence prevention curriculum and responsible citizenship should be integrated in the existing school curriculum. This should be throughout the academic curricula and include both experiential and cooperative learning strategies that focus on knowledge, skills, and values for dealing with and preventing school violence. Students should learn strategies to address personal safety, interpersonal communication, problem solving, anger management, and conflict resolution.
>
> *Early prevention efforts*: Policy efforts should guide staff and students toward early identification of school violence by ensuring that children at risk of bullying others or victims of bullying are identified and helped at the earliest possible stage. Identification should be followed up as soon as possible by intervention.
>
> *Procedures for dealing with violent incidents*: Policy should have guidelines for dealing with violent incidents that do not necessarily require involvement of the police, such as schoolyard fights that do not result in serious bodily harm; racial, cultural, or sexual harassment; and minor acts of vandalism.

It should also address more serious incidents of school violence or threats of violence and how to inform and involve local law enforcement. This should include the development and role of a crisis response team within the school setting.

> *Procedures for dealing with the aftermath of an incident:* Policy considerations should include safety and healing of the victims, the reentry of the perpetrator into the school system, and support and security of the witnesses.
>
> *Staff development:* School staff must be prepared for their role as prevention specialists as well as teachers and as facilitators of the resolution of conflicts. They must also know how and when to call on the support of others within both the school and the community. It is critical that staff be trained in conflict resolution and school violence prevention and management.
>
> *Student and parent involvement*: Open communication among parents or guardians, the school, and students is an important factor in ensuring the safety of the entire school community. Since many of the school shooters confided in the peers regarding their intentions, students can play a key role in violence prevention. Good rapport between the school and families allows problems to be addressed as early as possible, before they become serious.

Multidisciplinary Threat Assessment Team

A multidisciplinary threat assessment team begins with a threat assessment coordinator. The threat assessment coordinator could be a shared role between professionals. This person should oversee all assessments of threats of violence. This person could be the school administrator, school psychologist or counselor, mental health prevention worker, or any other staff who has had training is school threat assessment. The person would also need to have the authority to make quick independent decisions about school safety.

When a threat incident occurs, the staff who first becomes aware of the situation should report it to the threat assessment coordinator. The coordinator is then responsible for setting up the initial threat assessment, evaluating the threatener when identified, coordinating the intervention, and acting as liaison to other school staff, law enforcement personnel, and individuals from other social service agencies.

The multidisciplinary team would function in support of the activities directed by the coordinator. This team would include a variety of school staff and mental health professionals from either the school or a local mental health agency. From my experience, mental health agencies typically provide staff to serve on these teams as a volunteer member without cost to the school. It is strongly recommended that law enforcement also be a part of this team or at least be consulted on a regular basis.

Law Enforcement

The involvement of law enforcement in most cases is dependent on the level of threat. Threats that are low in risk (i.e., threats that are associated with temporary and quickly resolving emotional intensity) can often be resolved within the school setting. These likely do not need law enforcement intervention. Situations that are considered medium or high risk should include the guidance and involvement of law enforcement.

General Guidelines for Mediating Threats of Violence Based on Level of Risk

Schools typically will only mediate in situations of low- or medium-level threats that are directed at an individual. Generally, most medium- and all high-level threats are best left to law enforcement agencies, which are better equipped to deal with these situations. Following are some ideas identified by the Critical Incident Response Group, National Center for the Analysis of Violent Crime, and the FBI Academy (2005) in their report about violence in schools.

Mediating low-level risk is indicated when the person has been assessed to pose little threat to public or school safety. Typically, these situations have veiled or indirect statements of threat, and the threat content suggests that the student will not carry it out. These can be situations in which the student has expressed high-intensity emotions "in the moment" of the incident that dissipate following the incident, and the situation can be resolved in the office.

The student would be informed of the school policy and discipline code. The student would be given the opportunity for explanation. The student would then be discipline based on school policy.

Follow-up conversations would be necessary for all parents of the students involved. This would include the perpetrator, the potential victim, and the witnesses. It is important to remember mandated reporting laws and the need to inform all intended victims if they are identifiable. Those individuals would be notified of the potential threat and could be offered suggestions for keeping themselves safe.

Staff should meet with the student and his or her family to develop a specific plan for the threatener's return to school. The plan should include which security strategies will be put in place when the student returns. This could include strategies for additional monitoring in locations of the school during specific times of the day. Also included would be who is responsible for the security strategies.

The plan should also include which modifications are necessary in student schedules to accommodate the threatener's return. This would include any mental health groups or sessions that may need to be scheduled at school. Last, include identification of the necessary interventions that will take place at home. These are strategies that the parents will implement that address how the parents will supervise the student at home or in the community setting.

For low-level risk, there is usually no need to connect with law enforcement because the situation is resolved with the students involved, and the case is clear enough to determine that there is no criminal offense.

Medium-level risk is indicated when the threat poses a danger to school and community safety. Typically, these threats are more direct, specific, and plausible; there have been some thought and preparatory steps by the threatener. The threatener may have lasting emotional intensity, and the threat remains after the initial incident. High-level threat is direct, specific, and plausible, and there is a strong indication that steps have been taken by the threatener to carry out the plan.

Mediation for medium- and high-level threat would include the activation of the multidisciplinary team and contacting law enforcement. A response plan (prepared ahead of time) would be activated to make sure that all students and community are safe. Law enforcement would direct the intervention and would evaluate the threat for a criminal offense.

Considering that prevention matters, school staff should look to address the underlying cause of the threat. Often, students who threaten others or the school are experiencing school bullying or have other mental health concerns, such as depression, anxiety, or poor coping skills. Schools should consider the underlying causes as they relate to individual students and the school system as a whole.

8

PRACTICAL APPLICATION OF THE BULLYING LETHALITY IDENTIFICATION SYSTEM

Never be bullied into silence. Never allow yourself to be made a victim. Accept no one's definition of your life, but define yourself.

Harvey S. Firestone
Founder of the Firestone Tire and Rubber Company

Jacob: A Case of Bullying and Suicidal Ideation

Screen

Lisa called my private practice office to see if I would speak to a boy who was repeatedly being bullied on the bus while on the way home from school. Lisa worked at a local school as a mental health prevention specialist. She knew that I worked with bullying prevention and thought I might be able to offer some strategies to the 12-year-old to help him stop the bullying.

The following Thursday, I met with the boy and his parents. They were eager to tell me the details of the bullying that Jacob was experiencing. To help stay focused on the extent of the bullying, potential for suicidal ideation, and risk of school violence, I intended to follow the Bullying Lethality Screening Tool. Their explanation of the bullying situation made for an easy transition from their telling their story of bullying to my questions to assess the five indicators outlined on the Bullying Lethality Screening Tool.

Jacob shared that he was being bullied regularly by two brothers. The extent of the bullying was not exclusive to the bus, however. Sure, Damon and Marcus regularly teased and pushed him around on the bus, but the real challenge was the quarter mile walk from the bus stop down the gravel road that led to the boys' houses. On the walk, which often culminated in a run for Jacob to avoid the bullying, Jacob was pushed and teased, spit on, and occasionally when he chose to strike back, ended with Jacob being injured in some way.

As we talked, I asked questions related to the five dimensions of bullying identified on the Bullying Lethality Screening Tool. I rated bullying persistence and intensity high because the bullying occurred in two locations (the bus and the walk home); in combination, the bullying happened to some degree every day of the school week.

Jacob described having increased anxiety when he would get on the bus after school if the boys began teasing him. His fear would gradually increase as the bus neared his street because he suspected that some form of physical bullying would follow. Sometimes, the physical bullying would lead to a fight, so he did have some fear of being physically harmed. Jacob was effectively avoidant of the two boys, however, during school or during free time at home. Also, he could generally outrun them when the need presented itself. I rated him as moderate risk for coping responses.

Jacob was considered a nerd from a nerdy family by the boys who teased him. He was not involved with the boys who played sports and was more involved in academic pursuits such as chess club; the kids who teased him saw this as weird. Jacob was only accessible to the boys when he was transported home from school. The bullies did not really have access to Jacob in the neighborhood because their houses were fairly far apart, and they did not have interaction at school. Jacob planned to avoid the bullies and was fairly effective. I marked the screening tool as moderate for access and opportunity for escape (see Table 8.1).

The family began to discuss Jacob's concern for other family members. The family identified that the bullying did not stop with Jacob.

Table 8.1 Section: Bullying

Bullying Persistence and Intensity	Risk: High
Critical Item: Critical Coping Response	Risk: Moderate
Vulnerability	Risk: Low
Access	Risk: Moderate
Opportunity for Escape	Risk: Moderate

The bullies also seemed to be harassing Jacob's younger sister at school on the playground. Typically, they teased her about being from the "nerd" family and having the disease "nerdism." For Kelly, the teasing was distressing, but her typical response was to tell a teacher, and the teasing would stop. For Jacob, however, it was fairly upsetting that his little sister was being teased by the boys.

Curiously, Jacob's parents talked about the problems that they were having with the parents of the other boys. When Jacob's parents talked, I got the sense that they were being bullied by the other parents. I also wondered what bullying they might have done to the other family. From their description, the families have been "at war" for several years. Mostly, the war is fought by doing nasty pranks to each other that usually ended with one of the families calling the police on the other. The last incident for Jacob's family was having a dead snake placed in their mailbox and damage to the antenna of the family's pick-up truck.

I mentioned to Jacob that sometimes when kids experience bullying they also become sad. I told the family that I wanted to ask some questions that were specific to the symptoms of depression.

Jacob stated that he was not depressed. His parents were not sure that Jacob was being truthful. They stated that he lay around the house and was easily irritated by others' requests. They believed they could not ask him to do anything without him getting irritated. He did agree that he has little energy and just wants to relax when he gets home from school.

When we talked in further detail about depression, Jacob talked about not wanting to be identified as depressed and needing medicine; he was adamant about not being placed on medication. When I discussed with him that my reason for asking the question was not necessarily to prescribe medication but to assess the level of impact of bullying on his mental health, he readily agreed that he was sad most days. He also agreed with his parents that he was regularly irritable and did not know why. We talked about irritability as a potential indicator of depression in young people, which seemed to make sense to the family.

Jacob stated that he had no trouble with sleep and that he got plenty of sleep. His parents agreed, but only in that he sleeps a lot;

Table 8.2 Section: Depression

Critical Item: Depressed Mood	Risk: High
Sleep Disruption	Risk: Moderate
Loss of Energy	Risk: Moderate
Substance Use	Risk: Low
Hopelessness	Risk: Moderate
Concentration	Risk: Low

they believe that the sleep goes hand in hand with his lack of interest in doing anything other than lying around the house.

I determined that Jacob was depressed based on the answers to this section of the Bullying Lethality Screening Tool (Table 8.2). The critical item was marked, indicating further evaluation for depression. I was glad to hear that he was not using inappropriate coping strategies such as abusing alcohol or other drugs. This would certainly increase his risk level on both the depression and suicide sections of the screening tool. I advanced on the tool to consider suicidal ideation.

Jacob talked about how it was his fault for the bullying in his family. He seemed to take a deep responsibility for the "suffering" his family was experiencing, and his feelings to me seemed more like inappropriate guilt. He made the comment that sometimes he wondered if it would not be better if he were dead because that would relieve his family of the burden that he was causing. He said that he also imagined what his family would be like and how they would act if he were not around.

Although I considered his thoughts of death to be transient (i.e., they were occasional and probably more a symptom of depression), the screening tool indicates this as a Critical Item and a specific condition for further assessment, so I knew that it would be important to assess Jacob further for suicidal ideation. I did note that his thoughts seemed fairly organized, and he did not seem to have thoughts that were self-depreciating or supporting isolation, although his behavior was isolating and made me think that he may not have been forthcoming about his thinking patterns. He did have a strong sense of being a burden and had moderate ability to cope with the situation and generate solutions to the problem. I marked him as shown in Table 8.3 for suicidal ideation.

Table 8.3 Section: Suicidal Ideation

Critical Item: Thoughts of Death	Risk: High
Critical Item: Adult Concern	Risk: Low
Losses	Risk: Low
Coping	Risk: Moderate
Sense of Purpose	Risk: Low
Thinking Patterns	Risk: Moderate
Burdensomeness	Risk: Moderate

Table 8.4 Section: Isolation

Alienation by Peers	Risk: Low
Self-Alienation	Risk: Moderate
Family Connectedness	Risk: Low

Next, I focused by questioning about isolation (Table 8.4). I did not get the sense that Jacob had any peer difficulties other than those related to Damon and Marcus. He did do a fair amount of self-alienation, describing that he was contented and just wanted to relax and spend time reading in his room. His family disagreed and believed that he avoided everyone, and it was difficult to get him to leave his room.

The family seemed connected and did have a genuine concern and love for each other. There were some problems with appropriate discipline in that the parents seemed passive in their parenting style. Overall, parenting was not a concern.

There was no indication that Jacob made any threat to Damon or Marcus or toward the school. I did ask general questions regarding his desire to hurt Damon and Marcus or if he was angry with the school. He stated that he did not want to hurt anyone and only wanted the boys to stop bothering his family. I decided not to continue with the section on threat context and type and marked it nonapplicable.

Now that I had completed the Bullying Lethality Screening Tool, I believed that it was appropriate to continue with a suicide assessment because I wanted to understand the role of depression and the sense of burden that Jacob felt. Regardless of the outcome of the suicide assessment, I also wanted to refer him to counseling for further evaluation for depression. Counseling would also assist him in developing some strategies for assertively dealing with bullying behavior.

Assess

To start the assessment, I pulled out the BLIS Suicide Assessment and began to talk with Jacob in general terms about depression and thoughts of death. I asked him if he could give me more detail about his thoughts of death. He stated that he fantasized at times that he was dead or that he never existed, and he was able to see that his family got along better without him. He admitted that he had thought about suicide in the past but dismissed the idea a long time ago because he believed that he would go to hell if he committed suicide. This seemed to fit in with the family's faith.

There was no evidence that he had made any statements to family or friends about wanting to hurt himself or to attempt suicide. He also stated during the assessment that he did not want to die and really desired more to stop the bullying and shield his parents and sister from it. I marked all factors of the Intent and Lethality section of the assessment as low risk with the exception of Motivation for Escape, which I marked moderate because Jacob would like to escape the bullying and more so the burden he feels for his family.

Intent and Lethality	Communication of suicidal thought	☒ No ... ☐ Yes 0 1 2 3 4 5 6 7 8 9 10
	Desire for death	☒ Low ☐ Moderate ☐ High 0 1 2 3 4 5 6 7 8 9 10
	Prevention of detection	☒ Low ☐ Moderate ☐ High 0 1 2 3 4 5 6 7 8 9 10
	Evidence of planning	☒ No ☐ Yes 0 1 2 3 4 5 6 7 8 9 10
	Lethality of method available? ☐ Motivation for escape	☒ Low ☐ Moderate ☐ High 0 1 2 3 4 5 6 7 8 9 10 ☐ Low ☒ Moderate ☐ High 0 1 2 3 4 5 6 7 8 9 10

Thoughts: General thoughts of death. Thought of suicide in past. No communication of suicide intent or comments to others.

Plans: No plans.

Intent: Low level risk indicated by wish to escape. Otherwise no intent for self-harm.

Behaviors: No current or past suicidal behavior noted.

I asked Jacob about the family history of mental health and past suicidal behavior. He indicated that no one in his family had any mental health diagnosis or problems, and the family had no history of suicide attempts or suicidal ideation. I believed that the bullying was significant enough to consider it interpersonal conflict, so I marked that factor as elevated risk and marked the overall category as low risk.

History	
	☒ Interpersonal conflict
	☐ Recent loss
	☐ Previous suicide attempts
	☐ History of mental health diagnosis
	☐ Self-harming behavior
	☐ Family history of suicide health
	☐ Family history of mental health
	Overall Risk Level ☒ Low ☐ Moderate ☐ High

Jacob shared that he believed that he was a burden to his family, and that he wished that things would be better. He believed that his problems were causing problems for his sister and for his parents. He believed that the harassment the family was receiving from the other family was because he could not deal with Damon and Marcus.

When considering his mental status, I marked burdensome and depression as elevated risk on the assessment because of the information I had gathered on the screening tool. I also marked suicidal thought because he reported that he had thoughts of suicide in the past. I marked this overall category as moderate risk.

Mental Status	
	☒ Suicide or self-harm thoughts
	☒ Burdensome
	☐ Impulsivity
	☐ Hopelessness
	☒ Depression
	☐ Alcohol or other substance use
	☐ Panic attacks or anxiety
	☐ Thoughts, plans, intent for violence towards others
	Overall Risk Level ☐ Low ☒ Moderate ☐ High

I concluded that, overall, Jacob was low risk for attempting suicide in the immediate future. I did believe that he was depressed, and that if the depression and bullying continued, it would increase his risk.

I spoke with Jacob about some of the factors of the safety plan that seemed applicable and helpful for him. We discussed that if he were to have any suicidal thoughts in the future he should be honest with his parents and openly discuss this with them. He seemed open to this and said that he had done this before. We discussed the importance of connecting with others, and he agreed to reconnect with the youth group at his church.

Jacob needed to be better about connecting with others when he was upset. We decided that since he had a good connection with Lisa (the counselor who initially referred him), that he would go to her or call her if he needed help dealing with any crisis. I also recommended that he connect with a therapist for assessment and to continue seeing Lisa on a regular basis at school. I concluded the session with referral numbers for the family, the telephone number to the local crisis hotline, and a plan to follow up with the family in a couple of days.

Safety Plan	
	☒ Strategy to recognize and avert the potential crisis
	☒ Strategy for engaging social networks
	☐ Strategy for using internal coping strategies
	☐ Strategy for avoidance of risky situations
	☒ Strategy for utilizing positive support when troubled
	☒ Strategy for continuing treatment
	☐ Strategy for creating a safe environment
	☒ Strategy for knowing who to call

☒ Consulted/interaction with: ☐ Principal
                                        ☒ Other mental health professional
                                        ☐ Parent/Guardian
                                        ☐ Hospital
                                        ☐ Law enforcement
                                        ☐ Other_____

☐ Involved law enforcement. Outcome:_____
☐ Processed situation/feelings with student
☐ Collaborated with another agency_____
☐ No-harm contract created
☒ Crisis hotline number provided to student
☐ Hospitalization
☒ Mental health evaluation
☐ Other

Mediate

There was little mediation needed for suicidal behavior. I believed it was important to create a safety plan as a temporary strategy until Jacob could see a therapist on a regular basis. The plan for Jacob was initially to be assessed for depression and to receive mental health services.

Mediation for the bullying was important. I called the school to make sure that it was aware of the situation and asked the school to address the issues on the bus. The school staff stated that they would do this. I continued to see Jacob for six more sessions related to the bullying. We developed a goal to utilize friends to help with the situation. He was able to get two friends to make disapproving and distracting comments to Marcus and Damon when they teased him, and although this strategy was not my suggestion, it seemed to work to deflect the teasing on the bus.

We spent the rest of our time together practicing social skills that focused on assertive behavior, such as stopping the bullying or activating a bystander in the group, usually a friend. I wanted Jacob also to think realistically, so I told him that the skills do not always work because there are so many different circumstances that influence every situation. I suggested that staying with his friends as often as possible could support the success of his skills.

For any skill that I taught, I used the following format:

1. Introduce the skill and the reason for the skill
2. Teach the skill in steps
3. Counselor models the correct use of the skill
4. Client practices the skill with the counselor
5. Client receives positive feedback and critical suggestions from counselor

As an example, for one session, I wanted to teach how to stop aggressive behavior without Jacob having any intense emotional expression. First, I taught the skill in the following steps:

1. Recognize that what is happening is bullying and leave if possible
2. Notice emotions and try to limit this expression
3. Give strong eye contact, address the person in a firm tone, and state that you do not like what they are doing
4. Tell them to stop
5. Immediately walk away

An obvious conclusion is that this is a simple skill but a much harder task to pull off. Yet, beyond teaching a necessary skill, it opens for discussion the need to identify inappropriate aggressive behavior versus friendly teasing. Sometimes, kids are fairly sensitive to teasing, and it is important to make a judgment on the type of behavior that is displayed by a peer. The counselor is also able to support the idea that an intense emotional response by the victim is sometimes the thing that bullies want, and that by emotionally responding, the victim is in a way contributing to the problem. The skill gives three specific things to do: Tell the person that you do not like it, tell the person to stop, and immediately leave. This is the discussion I had as I was introducing the skill.

I taught the skill in steps and asked the client to give possible ways to act out the step. I followed by giving my own example. I then modeled the steps. When I had Jacob practice the steps, usually with me taking the role of the bully (but sometimes in family sessions, I will have other members play that part), I made sure to interrupt if the skill was not carried out properly for the first couple of attempts. Following the practice of the skill, I asked Jacob to give feedback on what he did well and what could use some work. I then gave my feedback.

David: A Case for Suicide and School Violence

Several years ago, I worked in a partial hospitalization program that took referrals from several local school districts in our community. I started at the inception of the program and witnessed the transformation from a program that saw a fair amount of violence directed between students and at staff to a much safer and more productive environment.

During those early days, I worked with a boy named David. David was from a small rural community about an hour from our facility, so he was bused to the facility. The community where he lived was mostly farming country and was culturally encapsulated. Unfortunately, there were several cases of incest in the community, and this caused it to garner the reputation in the mental health field as a community rampant with sexual relationships among family members.

David was isolated as well in his community; he was a rather large 17-year-old boy, weighing in at just about 300 pounds. He did not manage his hygiene well, which gave him a fairly pungent odor; coupled with his tendency to sweat excessively, that made him the favorite of other kids to tease and shun.

David had an interesting feature in that he had a "tell." Poker players will know the use of this word because a tell is a mannerism or movement that indicates that another player is bluffing. David's tell was what I would describe as a "snort and a push." He wore a large pair of glasses with rounded frames, and they would slide down his nose when it was lubricated by his sweat. When he had reached his breaking point, he would draw in a large, protracted breath through his nostrils while pushing his glasses up to the original position on his face with his middle finger.

All the children in the program were assigned a classroom for the school term and were required to attend one family and individual therapy session per week, along with instruction in a variety of academic subjects and therapeutic groups. David was assigned to Mrs. "T.'s" classroom; through the course of the year, this placement led him to believe that he could no longer bear living another day in her classroom. Mrs. T. was an accomplished bully to the children, probably rooted in her fear that the children would be aggressive and her need to control the environment she feared. David was a poor reader and had a low tolerance for frustration, but this teacher would regularly assign him worksheets to complete that brought him to his boiling point.

As children entered the program facility, they were checked at the front door for any contraband. On this particular day, David was discovered to have a portable music device and was asked to give it to us to hold until he left the program. He initially refused and stated to me that he believed that he could not face another day of his life if Mrs. T. was in it. We talked just briefly about the negativity of the statement, and I told him that we needed to continue with our check-in process. I assured him that I would let Mrs. T. know that I had his device, and that I would give him permission to take it to his family session. There, I thought that his counselor and mother could sort out David's noncompliance with the no contraband rule. Check-in continued with the other students, and David was escorted to the classroom by another employee.

When I was finished, I returned to the classroom and immediately felt an uncomfortable air about the room; I quickly noted that Mrs. T. was at her desk with her familiar stern and stoic look, and on the opposite end of the room was David standing facing her. I then became aware of my error, which was probably the antecedent to this standoff. Then came the tell, the snort and the push, and all eyes in the room turned to me in some final hope to quickly avert the pending outburst that would disrupt the room.

As if thought out and planned, David tore the telephone off the wall and hurled the phone directly at Mrs. T. with good dexterity; it landed somewhere past the right side of her head. As he did this, he moved toward her and began threatening to kill her. I told him to stop; he ignored me, and I got in front of him. Another staff member assisted from the other side, and we were able to divert him into a seclusion room.

In the seclusion room, David told staff that he was angry and felt hopeless that anything would change in the class, and that he would forever be at odds with his teacher, repeating that he did not know if he could face another day of his life if she were in it. He talked of his plan to drive to her home and kidnap her, take her to his farm, and torture her until she died.

After David had calmed down and had met the behavioral indicators that we had set for him to come out of the seclusion room, I walked with him to my office and began a more formal threat assessment. As a side note, screening was not indicated here because the threat of violence was the pressing issue that needed to be assessed immediately.

Assess

I would guess that about an hour passed between the time of the incident and David meeting me in my office. David was much calmer and had regained rationality. He was apologetic for his behavior and stated that he responded out of frustration that his teacher was not willing to listen to his concern for his electronic device or willing to agree to follow up with me about our conversation earlier in the morning. I also apologized for my contribution to the problem.

From this point, I began an unstructured interview with him using the BLIS Threat Assessment form. I completed the potentiating and precipitating factors and noted that some risk was indicated because he was male and had experienced ongoing bullying by his teacher that was associated with intense emotion at the time of the incident. I also know from my ongoing relationship that David that he had been diagnosed with major depressive disorder and was an occasional user of alcohol and marijuana. I knew that occasional substance use increases risk to some degree, and that depression is an important factor that increases risk.

Based on David's individual characteristics alone, in my judgment he was at moderate risk for carrying out the threat. He had low frustration tolerance due to the longevity of his current situation with his teacher. As we talked, I heard that he could identify alternative responses that he could have made in the classroom, so I did believe that he had some coping responses. I was also aware that he must have had some coping skills because he had managed to stay in the classroom with the teacher for months. David was not one who was fascinated with violent material or gaming, although his interest in the humor and excessive discussion of shows such as *South Park* could be unbearable at times.

Individual Characteristics	
☒	Signs of depression
☒	Low tolerance for frustration
☐	Poor coping responses
☐	Carries resentment and unwillingness to forgive wrongs by others
☐	Narcissism
☐	Lacks empathy
☐	Externalizes blame
☐	Intolerance
☒	Inappropriate humor
☐	Anger management problems
☐	Fascination with violent entertainment
☐	Vulnerability due to loss of relationship

Considering contextual factors, my concern was limited to David's relationship with his mother. His mother offered little guidance for him and on many occasions would wait for David to tell her what to do. School factors were only troubling in the sense that he was being bullied by his teacher, which I was aware was being addressed administratively with the teacher and was yet unresolved. His peer group had pretty much alienated him because of his hygiene and social skill deficits, which was a concern therapeutically yet not so much a concern for my threat assessment. Behaviorally, the only leakage that he presented was the in-the-moment threat to his teacher. None of the staff had concern for any of his conversations, drawings, or writing. For the contextual section, I considered him a mild risk.

Context	Family	☒ Problematic parent–child relationship ☒ Parents accept pathological behavior (lack reaction) ☐ Lack of intimacy ☐ Access to weapons ☐ Permissive/harsh parenting ☐ Child in charge
	School	☒ Detached from school ☐ Code of silence among students ☐ School culture has inadequate discipline/rigid rules ☐ Cliques ☒ Victim of persistent bullying ☒ Perceives others have inadequate response to bullying
	Peer Group	☐ Unlimited access to technology ☐ Peer group has or shares violent or extremist beliefs ☐ Negative influence ☐ Supports drug and alcohol use

David's threat was a direct threat stated and acted on in a moment of intense emotion. His threat did not have much plausibility to it because I knew that he had no transportation and could only get about with the assistance of his mother, who drove him when she could borrow a car from a neighbor. They lived in an impoverished community about an hour away from the community where the program was held, so there was little chance that he would walk to the program or to his teacher's home. He also did not know where she lived. His ability to follow her home from work was unlikely because his whereabouts were monitored from the time he left our facility to the time he stepped off the bus to go home. His threat was not persistent and did not last more than the time it took for him to reduce the intensity of his emotion, which I would guess was about an hour. I asked him how he might go about kidnapping his teacher to see if he would indicate any planned action steps, and he responded that he had not really thought about kidnapping her before the incident.

Threat Type: ☒ Direct ☐ Indirect ☐ Conditional ☐ Veiled			
Persistent Threat (lasting):	☐ Yes	☒ No	☐ To some degree
Plausible Threat:	☐ Yes	☒ No	☐ To some degree
Preparation:	☐ Yes	☒ No	☐ Undetermined

After the interview, I spoke with several of our staff and asked about any possible leakage, such as comments or writing that he had made regarding any hostility toward his teacher; all staff stated that they had no concerns. Thinking through all of the information available about the threat itself, I decide to indicate a low level for the Overall Risk Level of Threat section.

Overall Risk Level of Threat

☒ Low
    Threat vague and indirect, information about threat is inconsistent, implausible, and/or lacks detail
☐ Medium
    More direct and concrete, threatener has given some thought to plan (short of detailed plan), some preparatory steps
☐ High
    Threat is direct, specific, plausible; steps have been taken to carry out plan

Overall Contextual Support for Risk was moderate. He did not have a peer group who supported aggressive behavior or was focused on violent themes in music or gaming. Family factors seemed more of a clinical issue than a threat issue. The school, however, supported a high level of risk in that the school, the teacher, and David could not change the dynamic among the three. As I thought of his behavior, I had to rank this as medium. The direction of risk is at his teacher yet there is no indicated time or place that an attack will happen in the future.

Overall Contextual Support for Risk			
	Interviewer Judgment		
Individual characteristics indicate risk	☐ Low	☒ Medium	☐ High
Family context indicates risk	☒ Low	☐ Medium	☐ High
School context indicates risk	☐ Low	☐ Medium	☒ High
Peer group indicates risk	☒ Low	☐ Medium	☐ High
Behavior indicates risk	☐ Low	☒ Medium	☐ High
Risk Direction			
What: Threat to kidnap teacher and torture her Where: At his farm When: Unidentified Whom: Teacher			

Mediate

Based on program policy, David was disciplined for his aggressive behavior. He returned to class and was able to be productive the rest of the day. Several follow-up sessions were conducted by the family therapist to ensure that the assessment was accurate and that David was not having any persistent thoughts of harming his teacher. Local law enforcement was consulted, and no charges were filed against David. He was told that any further threat would be reported to the police and could lead to prosecution.

In this situation, there was also a systemic issue that contributed to the problem. The teacher was disciplined, and training was conducted for the staff on how to recognize bullying and the reporting procedures that were expected. A few months following David's threat, Mrs. T. resigned. Later, I learned that she had taken a position and was still working in the public school system.

Epilogue

I never had the pleasure of meeting Desire´ Dreyer, the girl whose death set me in motion to write this book. I got to know her as I spoke with the staff at her school and through interviews with her mother. Desire´ was the kind of person who would have done anything for anyone; her mother described her as having a heart of gold. In the final years of her short life, she went through a rough time; most of it she kept secret. She was tormented by those who at one time she considered friends. Ultimately, she ended her life to escape the pain. Those who miss her still post notes on her MySpace page.

After Desire´'s suicide, the school district made many changes in their system to address the problem of bullying. The school began by implementing the Olweus Bullying Prevention program at the campuses of their two high and middle schools. The following year, they began an aggressive implementation of bullying prevention. In total, they implemented the Olweus program in all 12 of their schools, which included 8 elementary, 2 middle, and 2 high schools.

Their efforts would not have happened without the support of the county's Mental Health and Recovery Board and the local Family and Children First (FCF) Council. These two entities provided grant funding for most of the training and material cost of the program. This was no small amount of money. The board and FCF did not stop there. For several years, they continued to provide funding for this district and several other school districts to implement bullying prevention. These programs continue today.

As for me, I collected data at the high schools mentioned at the beginning of the book and received my doctorate. At the same time, I began writing this book. With my friend and colleague Susan Graham from Child Focus Incorporated, I developed the Bullying Lethality Screening Tool and began to share it with professionals across the country. Recently, I left Child Focus. I am currently teaching full time at Xavier University in Cincinnati, Ohio.

The work continues. I continue to travel and speak about the devastating impact of bullying on the mental health of our children. As I write, a school district in Mentor, Ohio, is the subject of a lawsuit and is being highlighted in the local media for four suicides related to bullying in their district between 2006 and 2008. Ken Meyers, the attorney for the families, said that the school took a laissez-faire approach to addressing the bullying. In November 2010, Susan and I were able to offer a workshop in this community and share the Bullying Lethality Identification System (BLIS) with mental health professionals.

We all need to stand up and be counted on this issue; communities must have guidance and support from their leaders, schools need to intervene immediately for the safety of students, parents need to partner with their children's school, and students must not be silent. None of us should look the other way when a disenfranchised kid is teased or alienated from peers. When students feel safe, they will report bullying behavior, and they will be less concerned about the social impact of their school relationships and more focused on their education.

I am proud of the Clermont County, Child Focus, Inc., the West Clermont School District, and my work with Susan Graham. Their investment in the safety and wellness of our community's children has been commendable. The numbers speak for themselves. In total, we have implemented bullying prevention in 41 schools, 30 within our own county, with an impact on roughly 16,000 students in our districts.

The bullies took her life away from me
I do not know if I can ever forgive.
I'm angry. How can they continue with theirs?
Their parents will see them attend senior prom,
Walk across the stage at graduation
Get married and embrace their grandchildren.
Now all I have are memories;
I long to see her smile,
I long to hear her attitude.
She is not here to
Give chocolate milk to in the mornings,
Sing songs in the afternoon,
Or beg for money to go to the movies in the evening.
Instead, I now have an empty home;
Laughter is lost;
Silence is overwhelming.
Her car sits in the garage
Waiting for her to drive down our street;
Windows down
Hair blowing in the wind.
Her room sits the way she left it
Waiting for her return.
I too lose track of reality;
To think that at any minute
She will come through our front door.

Donna Dreyer

References

Act now to stop a suicide. What to look for—and what to do—if you are concerned about someone. Questionnaire. Retrieved June 25, 2010, from http://www.stopasuicide.org

American Psychiatric Association. (2000). *Diagnostic and statistical manual of mental disorders* (4th ed., text revision). Washington, DC: Author.

Austin. S., & Joseph, S. (1996). Assessment of bully/victim problems in 8– to 11– year-olds. *British Journal of Educational Psychology, 66*, 447–456.

Baldry, A. C., & Farrington, D. P. (2000). Bullies and delinquents: Personal characteristics and parental styles. *Journal of Community and Applied Social Psychology, 10*, 17–31.

Barboza, G. E.., Schiamberg, L. B., Oehmke, J., Korzeniewski, S. J., Post, L. A., & Heraux, C. G. (2009). Individual characteristics and the multiple contexts of adolescent bullying: An ecological perspective. *Journal of Youth Adolescence,38*, 101–121.

Bertolote, J. M., & Fleischmann, A. (2010). *Suicide and psychiatric diagnosis: A worldwide perspective* (Mental health policy paper). Geneva, Switzerland: Department of Mental Health and Substance Dependence, World Health Organization. Retrieved September 16, 2010, from http://www.ncbi.nlm.nih.gov/pmc/articles/PMC1489848/pdf/wpa010181.pdf

Blaauw, E., Winkel, F. W., & Kerkhof, A. (2001). Bullying and suicidal behavior in jails. *Criminal Justice and Behavior, 28*, 279–299.

Bowers, L., Smith, P. K., and Binney, V. A. (1992). Cohesion and power in the families of children involved in bully/victim problems at school. *Journal of Family Therapy, 14*, 371–387.

Bridge, J. A., Goldstein, T. R., and Brent, D. A. (2006). Adolescent suicide and suicidal behavior. *Journal of Child Psychology and Psychiatry, 47*, 372–394.

Bronfenbrenner, U. (1977). Toward an experimental ecology of human development. *American Psychologist, 32*, 513–531.

Brown, S., & Taylor, K. (2008). Bullying, education and earnings: Evidence from the national child development study. *Economics of Educational Review, 27*, 387–401.

Carter, G. (2010). *Early warning, timely response: A guide to safe schools: The referenced edition.* Retrieved June 14, 2010, from http://cecp.air.org/guide/annotated.asp#Letter

Child Abuse Prevention and Treatment Act 2003: As amended by the Keeping Children and Families Safe Act of 2003. U.S. Department of Health and Human Services: Administration for Children and Families; Administration on Children Youth and Families; Children's Bureau; and the Office on Child Abuse and Neglect. June 25, 2003.

Connolly, I. & O'Moore, M. (2003). Personality and family relations of children who bully. *Personality and Individual Differences, 35*, 559-567.

Conyne, R. K., & Cook, E. P. (2004). *Ecological counseling: An innovative approach to conceptualizing person-environment interaction.* Alexandria, VA: American Counseling Association.

Cray, D. (2010, March). Decrease seen in children's bullying. *Cincinnati Enquirer* via Associated Press.

Critical Incident Response Group, National Center for the Analysis of Violent Crime and the FBI Academy. (2005). *The school shooter: A threat assessment perspective.* Quantico, VA: FBI Academy.

Cutter, F. (2010). *Prediction and the need for practical assessment.* Retrieved June 30, 2010, from http://www.suicidepreventtriangle.org

Dake, J. A., Price, J. H., & Telljohawn, S. K. (2003). The nature and extent of bullying at school. *Journal of School Health, 74*(5), 173–180.

Davis, S., & Davis, J. (2007). *Empowering bystanders in bullying prevention.* Champaign, IL: Research Press.

Department of Education and Early Childhood Development. (2009). *Strategies for parents.* Retrieved April 18, 2010, from http://www.education.vic.gov.au/healthwellbeing/safety/bullying/goodpractice/parentstrategy.htm

Duncan, R. D. (1999). Maltreatment by parents and peers: The relationship between child abuse, bullying victimization and psychological distress. *Child Maltreatment, 4*, 45–55.

Durlak, J. A., & Wells, A. M. (1997). Primary prevention mental health programs for children and adolescents: A meta-analytic review. *American Journal of Community Psychology, 25*, 115-152.

Dussich, J. P. J., & Maekoya, C. (2007). Physical child harm and bullying-related behaviors: A comparative study in Japan, South Africa and the United States. *International Journal of Offender Therapy and Comparative Criminology, 51*, 495–504.

Elgar, F. J., Craig, W., Boyce, W., Morgan, A., & Vella-Zarb, R. (2009). Income inequality and school bullying: Multilevel study of adolescents in 37 countries. *Journal of Adolescent Health, 45*, 351–359.

Fekkes, M., Pijpers, F. M., & Verloove-Vanhorick, P. (2004). Bullying behavior and associations with psychosomatic complaints and depression in victims. *The Journal of Pediatrics, 1*, 17–22.

Firestone, R. W., & Catlett, J. (2009). *Beyond death anxiety: Achieving life affirming death awareness.* New York: Springer Publishing.

Flouri, E., & Buchanan, A. (2003). The role of mother involvement and father involvement in adolescent bullying behavior. *Journal of Interpersonal Violence, 18*, 634–644.

Georgiou, S. N. (2008). Bullying and victimization: The role of mothers. *British Journal of Educational Psychology, 78*, 109–125.

Glew, G., Rivara, F., & Feudtner, C. (2000). Bullying: Children hurting children. *Pediatrics in Review, 21*(6), 183–189.

Goldstein, A. P., Sprafkin, R. P., Gershaw, N. J., & Klein, P. (1980). *SkillStreaming the adolescent: A structured learning approach to teaching prosocial skills.* Champaign, IL: Research Press.

Graham, S., & Losey, B. (2006). *Signs of suicide program: Preliminary results.* Report for the West Clermont School District and Child Focus Incorporated. Cincinnati, OH: Child Focus Incorporated.

Granello, P., & Granello, D. (2008, January). *Advancing your suicide prevention, assessment, and intervention skills: Practical information for counselors.* Presentation Information and Resources presented at the Greater Cincinnati Counseling Association's Annual Conference, Cincinnati, OH.

Guo, B., & Harstall, C. (2004). *For which strategies of suicide prevention is there evidence of effectiveness?* (Health Evidence Network report). Copenhagen, Denmark: WHO Regional Office for Europe. Retrieved June 25, 2010, from http://www.euro.who.int/Document/E83583.pdf

Harlow, H. (1958). The nature of love. *American Psychologist, 13*, 573–685.

Harvard School of Public Health. (2010). Means matter: Method, choice, intent. Retrieved July 1, 2010, from http://www.hsph.harvard.edu/means-matter/means-matter/intent/index.html

Hawkins, L. D., Pepler, D. J., & Craig, W. M. (2001). Naturalistic observation of peer interventions in bullying. *Social Development, 10*, 512–527.

Jacobs, D. G. (1999). Depression screening as an intervention against suicide. *Journal of Clinical Psychiatry, 60* (Supplement 2), 42–45.

Johnson, M. (2006). The social world of children: Strategies for handling annoying bullying and teasing. A guide for parents in helping their children deal with bullies, meanies, and teasers. Adapted from Orpinas, P., & Horne, A. (2005). *Bullying prevention: Creating a positive school climate and developing social competence.* Washington, DC: American Psychological Association.

Johnston, D. (2007). Excerpt. In B. High (Compiler), *Bullycide in America.* Retrieved December 3, 2009, from http://www.bullycide.org

Joiner, T. (2007). *Why people die by suicide.* Cambridge, MA: Harvard University Press.

Kienhorst, I. C., De Wilde, E. J., Diekstra, R. F., & Wolters, W. H. (1995). Adolescents' image of their suicide attempt. *Journal of the American Academy of Child and Adolescent Psychiatry, 34*, 623–628.

Kokkinos, C., & Panayiotou, G. (2004). Predicting bullying and victimization among early adolescents: Associations with disruptive behavior disorders. *Aggressive Behavior, 30*, 520–534.

Kronenberger, W. G., & Meyer, R. G. (1996). *The child clinician's handbook.* Boston: Allyn and Bacon.

Kumpulainen, K., Rasanen E., & Puura, K. (2001). Psychiatric disorders and the use of mental health services among children involved in bullying. *Aggressive Behavior, 27*, 102–110.

Lewin, K. (1936). *Principals of topological psychology.* New York: McGraw-Hill.

Limber, S., Mullin-Rindler, N., Riese, J., Flerx, V., & Snyder, M. (2004). *The Olweus bullying prevention program coordinating committee training. Olweus Bullying Prevention Group.* Clemson, SC: Clemson University.

Lober, R., & Tengs, T. (1986). The analysis of coercive chains between children, mothers and siblings. *Journal of Family Violence, 1*(1), 51–70.

Losey, B., & Graham, S. (2004). *The scope of bullying behavior in rural school communities: A survey of elementary students in Clermont County, Ohio. Community report.* Cincinnati, OH: Child Focus Incorporated.

Lund, R., Nielsen, K. K., Hansen, D. H., Kriegbaum, M., Molbo, D., Due, P., & Christensen, U. (2008). Exposure to bullying at school and depression in adulthood: A study of Danish men born in 1953. *European Journal of Public Health, 19*, 111–116.

Maton, K. (1999). Making a difference: The social ecology of social transformation. *American Journal of Community Psychology, 28*, 1.

McGlothlin, J. (2007). *Developing clinical skills in suicide assessment, prevention, and treatment.* Alexandria, VA: American Counseling Association.

McMyler, C., & Pryjmachuk, S. (2008). Do "no-suicide" contracts work? *Journal of Psychiatric and Mental Health Nursing, 15*, 512–522.

Nansel, T. R., Overpeck, M., Pilla, R. S., Ruan, W. J., Simons-Morton, B., & Scheidt, P. (2001). Bullying behaviors among U.S. youth: Prevalence and association with psychosocial adjustment. *Journal of the American Medical Association, 285*(16): 2094-2100.

Naparstek, A. J. (1999). Community building and social group work: A new practice paradigm for American cities. In H. Bertcher, L.F. Kurtz & A. Lamont (Eds). *Rebuilding communities challenges for group work* (pp. 17-33). New York: Haworth Press.

Office of Applied Studies. (2002). *The NHSDA Report. Substance use and the risk of suicide among youths.* Rockville, MD: Substance Abuse and Mental Health Services Administration. Retrieved December 15, 2010 from http://www.oas.samhsa.gov/2k2/suicide/suicide.htm

Oliver, C., & Candappa, M. (2003). *Tackling bullying: Listening to the views of children and young people* (Research Report RR400, Department of Education and Skills). London: Thomas Corham Research Unit, Institute of Education.

Olweus, D. (1989). Peer relationship problems: Conceptual issues and a successful intervention program against bully/victim problems. Paper presented at the symposium on "aggressors, victims and peer relationships." Kansas City, USA, April 27-30.

Olweus, D. (1993). *Bullying at school: What we know and what we can do.* Oxford, UK: Wiley-Blackwell.

Olweus, D. (2001). General information about the revised Olweus bully/victim questionnaire, PC Program and Teacher Handbook. Retrieved December 6, 2008, from http://www.ed.gov/admins/lead/safety/training/bullying/question.pdf.

Olweus, D., Limber, S., Mullin-Rindler, N., Riese, J., Flerx, V., & Snyder, M. (2005). *The Olweus bullying prevention program coordinating committee training manual.* Clemson University.

O'Moore, M. (2000). Critical issues for teacher training to counter bullying and victimisation in Ireland. *Aggressive Behavior, 26*, 99-111.

O'Moore, M., & Kirkham, C. (2001). Self-esteem and its relationship to bullying behaviour. *Aggressive Behavior. 27*(4): 269-283.

Ontario Ministry of Education. (2008). Violence-free schools policy. Retrieved July 4, 2010, from http://www.edu.gov.on.ca/eng/document/policy/vfreeng.html

Pepler, D. J., & Craig, W. (2000). *Making a difference in bullying.* Retrieved September 12, 2010, from http://www.melissainstitute.org/documents/MakingADifference.pdf

Pinderhughes, E. E., Dodge, K. A., Bates, J. E., Pettit, G. S., & Zelli, A. (2000). Discipline responses: Influences of parents' socioeconomic status, ethnicity, beliefs about parenting, stress, and cognitive-emotional processes. *Journal of Family Psychology, 14*, 380–400.

Rigby, K. (1994). Psychosocial functioning in families of Australian adolescent schoolchildren involved in bully/victim problems. *Journal of Family Therapy, 16*, 173–187.

Rigby, K. (1996). *Bullying in schools: And what to do about it.* Briston, PA: Kingsley.

Rivers, I., & Noret, N. (2010). Participant roles in bullying behavior and their association with thoughts of ending one's life. *Crisis, 31*(3), 143–148.

Schreier, A., Wolke, D., Thomas, K., Horwood, J., Hollis, C., Gunnell, D., et al. (2009). Prospective study of peer victimization in childhood and psychotic symptoms in a nonclinical population at age 12 years. *Archives of General Psychiatry, 66*, 527–536.

Shepherd J. P., & Farrington D. P. (1995). Preventing crime and violence. *British Medical Journal, 310*, 271–272.

Solberg, M. E., Olweus, D., & Endresen, I. M. (2007). Bullies and victims at school: Are they the same pupils? *British Journal of Educational Psychology, 77*, 441–464.

Spriggs, A. L., Iannotti, R. J., Nansel, T. R., & Haynie, D. L. (2007). Adolescent bullying involvement and perceived family, peer and school relations: Commonalities and differences across race/ethnicity. *Journal of Adolescent Health, 41*, 283–293.

Stanley, B., & Brown, G. K. (2008). *Safety plan treatment manual to reduce suicide risk: Veteran version.*

State of Victoria Department of Education and Early Childhood Development. Safe schools: A strategy for parents. Retrieved February 11, 2011 from http://www.eduweb.vic.gov/au/edulibrary/public/stuman/wellbeing/SS_Parents_factsheet_English.pdf

Stossel, J. (2001). The in crowd and social cruelty [VHS video, television series episode]. In *20/20.* ABC News Productions Broadcast of February 15, 2002.

Stueve, A., Dash, K., O'Donnell, L., Tehranifar, P., Wilson-Simmons, R., Slaby, R., et al. (2006). Rethinking the bystander role in school violence prevention. *Health Promotion Practice, 7*(1), 117–124.

Tanaka, T. (2001). The identity formation of the victim of "shunning." *School Psychology International, 22,* 463–476.

U.S. Department of Health and Human Services. (2008). *Child maltreatment: Annual report.* Retrieved June 11, 2009, from www.acf.hhs.gov/programs/cb/stats_research/index.htm#can

Van der Wal, M. F., de Wit, C. A., & Hirasing, R. A. (2003). Psychosocial health among young victims and offenders of direct and indirect bullying. *Pediatrics, 111,* 1312–1317.

Whitney, I., & Smith, P. K. (1991). A survey of the nature and extent of bully/victim problems in junior/middle and secondary schools. *Educational Resources, 35,* 3–25.

Wolfe, D. A., Crooks, C. C., & Jaffe, P. (2009). Child maltreatment, bullying, gender-based harassment and adolescent dating violence: Making the connection. *Psychology of Women Quarterly, 33,* 21–24.

Wolke, D., Woods, S., Bloomfield, L., & Karstadt, L. (2000). The association between direct and relational bullying and behavior problems among primary school children. *Journal of Child Psychological Psychiatry 41,* 989–1002.

Appendix A: Bullying Lethality Screening Tool

Bullying Lethality Screening Tool

BULLYING

	LOW RISK	MODERATE RISK	HIGH RISK
Bullying Persistence and Intensity		Bullied at least weekly, on a consistent basis	Persistent bullying every day, on a consistent basis
CRITICAL ITEM:* Critical Coping Responses		Moderate physical or emotional harm to child	Real/Perceived Threat of Bodily Harm or Death Highly Anxious, Fearful, Avoidant
Vulnerability of target		Target is viewed as different from peers, difference is viewed negatively and it is used against him/her	Target is viewed as different than peers, difference is viewed negatively and it is used to hurt them. Target has limited resiliency and coping responses
Access to target		Target is accessible in multiple environments, yet target has some skills to block or avoid bullying	Accessible almost all of the time via technology (phone, IM, text, etc.) or physical contact
Target's perceived opportunity to escape		Avoiding bullying takes action and planning on part of target	Impossible/difficult to escape the bully

SUBTOTAL ☐

DEPRESSION

	LOW RISK	MODERATE RISK	HIGH RISK
CRITICAL ITEM*			Feeling down or depressed most of the day, every day (may present as irritability, anxiety, or empty mood in children) OR loss of interest or pleasure in everyday activities
Sleep Disruption	No difficulty or very intermittent difficulties with sleep	Unusual sleeping patterns (nocturnal wakefulness or excessively)	Persistent unusual patterns in sleeping (nocturnal wakefulness or excessive sleep)
Loss of Energy	No evidence of fatigue or low energy	Fatigue experience several times per week	Chronic fatigue
Substance Use	No use or some experimentation with substances	Family or personal history of substance use	Regular/frequent use as coping strategy or binge use
Hopelessness	No sense of hopelessness	Feeling hopeless, helpless, or inappropriate guilt at times	Persistent hopelessness about self and future. Feelings of failure, letting self or family down
Concentration	Little to no difficulty concentrating	Trouble concentrating 2–4 times per week	Consistent trouble concentrating on tasks, daily

SUBTOTAL ☐

ISOLATION by Self and Others

	LOW RISK	MODERATE RISK	HIGH RISK
Alienation by Peers	Student has a solid group of friends, good friendship skills, and potential defenders	Weakening inhibition of other students about student being bullied. Others join in on bullying	Student appears isolated from peers, has no friends and minimal skills for developing friendships
Self-Alienation		Spends time in room, not interested in activities. Limits involvement with family and friends	Negative self-loathing thoughts expressed in comments to others and frequent isolating behavior
Family Connectedness	Family life provides high levels of love and support. Positive communication	Negative communication, problematic discipline	Negative or hostile communication, problematic parenting techniques, inadequate parent responsiveness to child's needs

SUBTOTAL ☐

* CRITICAL ITEMS must be given immediate attention.

SUICIDAL IDEATION	LOW RISK	MODERATE RISK	HIGH RISK
CRITICAL ITEM*			Thoughts of being better off dead or thoughts of hurting self in some way
CRITICAL ITEM*			Adult concerned about this individual's likelihood to harm self or others if no intervention occurs
Losses	No losses experienced	Recent loss, high emotional arousal	Recent loss coupled with high emotional arousal, impulsivity, and suicide ideation
Coping	Able to cope with stressors. Daily activities continue as usual with little change	Some difficulty regulating emotions, difficulty generating solutions	Intense emotion, difficulty regulation emotion, immobile thinking. Unable to generate solutions.
Sense of Purpose	Sense of purpose in life	Questions his/her purpose in life	No sense of purpose in life or connection to activities that offer meaning.
Thinking Patterns	Organized, clear, realistic view of self (negative/positive)	Self-depreciating thoughts, thoughts influencing isolation.	Self-annihilating thoughts.
Burdensomeness	NOT a burden to others	Some sense of burdensomeness to others & somewhat ineffective in resolving this feeling	Perceives that their existence is a burden to others and others would be better off with them dead
SUBTOTAL			

Threat Context and Type	LOW RISK	MODERATE RISK	HIGH RISK
Persistent	Veiled threat, no intent to follow through	Threat is a temporary expression of anger, frustration, etc.	Intent to harm beyond the immediate situation
Plausible	Vague, indirect	Some thought given to how to carry out threat	Detailed threat, logical, identified target, strong potential for follow through
Preparation	No preparation, no realism	Possible place and time, no indication of practicing, leakage	Developmental signpost, leakage, practice, detailed and specific
Motivation	Low emotional arousal	Temporary expressions of anger and frustration; takes responsibility	Intent to physically harm beyond immediate situation, serious threats to kill, injure, or sexually violate
SUBTOTAL			

GRAND TOTAL	LOW RISK	MODERATE RISK	HIGH RISK

Scoring Instructions: Use check marks to indicate level of risk in each category. Calculate a subtotal in each of the 5 sections, then add each column to determine the grand total for each risk level.

Student Name:

Interviewer Signature:

Date:

Dr. Butch Losey, his staff and agents, shall not be liable for claims or damages and expressly disclaims any and all liability of any nature for any action, or nonaction, taken as a result of the information generated by the BLIS Screening Tool. Results from the BLIS Screening Tool are not diagnostic, but merely indicate the presence, or lack thereof, of symptoms that are consistent, or inconsistent with depression, suicidality, or homicidality. Negative responses to the questionnaires do not rule out risk, and positive responses do not conclusively establish suicidality or homicidality. A diagnostic evaluation by a healthcare professional is always necessary to determine whether or not there is the presence/absence of depression/suicidality/homicidality.

Appendix B: Suicide Assessment

Bullying Lethality Identification System

Student Name: Date of Birth:

Assessment Date:

Person Completing Assessment:

Exact Threat:

	Strength of Intent

Intent and Lethality

Communication of suicidal thoughts

☐ No   ☐ Yes

0 1 2 3 4 5 6 7 8 9 10

Desire for death

☐ Low   ☐ Moderate   ☐ High

0 1 2 3 4 5 6 7 8 9 10

Prevention of detection

☐ Low   ☐ Moderate   ☐ High

0 1 2 3 4 5 6 7 8 9 10

Evidence of planning

☐ No   ☐ Yes

0 1 2 3 4 5 6 7 8 9 10

Lethality of method available? ☐

☐ Low   ☐ Moderate   ☐ High

0 1 2 3 4 5 6 7 8 9 10

Motivation for escape

☐ Low   ☐ Moderate   ☐ High

0 1 2 3 4 5 6 7 8 9 10

Thoughts:

Plans:

Intent:

Behaviors:

History	☐ Interpersonal conflict ☐ Recent loss ☐ Previous suicide attempts ☐ History of mental health diagnosis ☐ Self-harming behavior ☐ Family history of suicide health ☐ Family history of mental health Overall Risk Level ☐ Low ☐ Moderate ☐ High

Mental Status	☐ Suicide or self-harm thoughts ☐ Burdensome ☐ Impulsivity ☐ Hopelessness ☐ Depression ☐ Alcohol or other substance use ☐ Panic attacks or anxiety ☐ Thoughts, plans, intent for violence towards others Overall Risk Level ☐ Low ☐ Moderate ☐ High

Response

Safety Plan	☐ Strategy to recognize and avert the potential crisis ☐ Strategy for engaging social networks ☐ Strategy for using internal coping strategies ☐ Strategy for avoidance of risky situations ☐ Strategy for utilizing positive support when troubled ☐ Strategy for continuing treatment ☐ Strategy for creating a safe environment ☐ Strategy for knowing who to call

☐ Consulted/interaction with: ☐ Principal
☐ Other mental health professional
☐ Parent/Guardian
☐ Hospital
☐ Law enforcement
☐ Other _____

☐ Involved law enforcement. Outcome:_____
☐ Processed situation/feelings with student
☐ Collaborated with another agency _____
☐ No-harm contract created
☐ Crisis hotline number provided to student
☐ Hospitalization
☐ Mental Health Evaluation
☐ Other

Notes

Appendix C: Threat Assessment

Bullying Lethality Identification System

Student Name: Date of Birth:

Assessment Date:

Person Completing Assessment:

Exact Threat:

Assessment of Individual		
	Potentiating Factors	Precipitation Factors
Demographics	☐ Diagnosis_____ ☐ Male Gender ☐ Substance Use ☐ Depression	☐ Intense feelings due to crisis ☐ Feeling bullied or victimized ☐ Others (indicate):
Individual Characteristics	☐ Signs of depression ☐ Low tolerance for frustration ☐ Poor coping responses ☐ Carries resentment and unwillingness to forgive wrongs by others ☐ Narcissism ☐ Lacks empathy ☐ Externalizes blame ☐ Intolerance ☐ Inappropriate humor ☐ Anger management problems ☐ Fascination with violent entertainment ☐ Vulnerability due to loss of relationship	
Context — Family	☐ Problematic parent–child relationship ☐ Parents accept pathological behavior (lack reaction) ☐ Lack of intimacy ☐ Access to weapons ☐ Permissive/harsh parenting ☐ Child in charge	
Context — School	☐ Detached from school ☐ Code of silence among students ☐ School culture has inadequate discipline/rigid rules ☐ Cliques ☐ Victim of persistent bullying ☐ Perceives others have inadequate response to bullying	
Context — Group	☐ Unlimited access to technology ☐ Peer group has or shares violent or extremist beliefs ☐ Negative influence ☐ Supports drug and alcohol use	
Behavior	☐ Leakage present (intentional or unintentional cues to feeling, thoughts, fantasies, attitudes, and intentions) ☐ Concerning conversations, drawings, writings ☐ History of aggression towards others/violent behavior ☐ Behavior relevant to carrying out threat (practicing with handguns, frequenting violent Web sites)	

Assessment of Threat

Threat Type:
☐ Direct
☐ Indirect
☐ Conditional
☐ Veiled

Persistent Threat (lasting):	☐ Yes	☐ No	☐ To some degree
Plausible Threat:	☐ Yes	☐ No	☐ To some degree
Preparation:	☐ Yes	☐ No	☐ Undetermined

Overall Risk Level of Threat

☐ Low
    Threat vague and indirect, information about threat is inconsistent, implausible, and/or lacks detail
☐ Medium
    More direct and concrete, threatener has given some thought to plan (short of a detailed plan), some preparatory steps
☐ High
    Threat is direct, specific, plausible; steps have been taken to carry out plan

Overall Contextual Support for Risk

Interviewer Judgment

Individual characteristics indicates risk	☐ Low	☐ Medium	☐ High
Family context indicates risk	☐ Low	☐ Medium	☐ High
School context indicates risk	☐ Low	☐ Medium	☐ High
Peer group indicates risk	☐ Low	☐ Medium	☐ High
Behavior indicates risk	☐ Low	☐ Medium	☐ High

Risk Direction

What:
Where:
When:
Whom:

Response

☐ Activated Multidisciplinary Team

☐ Consulted/discussion with: ☐ Law enforcement
                              ☐ Principal
                              ☐ Mental health professional
                              ☐ Parent/Guardian
                              ☐ Other_____

☐ Involved law enforcement. Outcome: _____
☐ Processed situation/feelings with student
☐ Collaborated with another agency_____
☐ Intended victim notified_____
☐ Crisis hotline number provided to student
☐ Hospitalization
☐ Mental Health Evaluation
☐ Other

Notes

Appendix D: Documentation of Bullying Intervention

Bullying Lethality Identification System

Date:
Students Involved:
Situation:

Screening

Bullying lethality screening measure administered and date:
Indication of screening measure:

Assessment

Suicide assessment administered and date:
Indications of suicide assessment:
Threat assessment administered and date:
Indications of threat assessment:

Mediation

Parent notification (indicate who, when, and how: collaboration efforts with the parent):

Staff response to bullying:

Plan of action for bullying:

    1. Goal:

        Objective:

        Implementation date: Follow-up date:

    2. Goal:

        Objective:

        Implementation date: Follow-up date:

Mediation Plan

Teach structured social skills

Develop in-the-moment strategies

Teach assertive behavior

Develop strategies for activating the bystanders

Help parents intervene

Impact of resiliency factors

Documentation of Follow-up

Date of follow-up:

Student:

Parent:

Other:

Outcome of follow-up:

Index

CD Contents